PRAIRIE UP

3 FIELDS BOOKS
An imprint of the University of Illinois Press

PRAIRIE UP

An Introduction to Natural Garden Design

BENJAMIN VOGT

3 Fields Books is an imprint of the University of Illinois Press.

Manufactured in the United States of America
P 10 9 8 7 6
∞ This book is printed on acid-free paper.

Library of Congress Cataloging-in-Publication Data
Names: Vogt, Benjamin, author.
Title: Prairie up : an introduction to natural garden design / Benjamin Vogt.
Other titles: Introduction to natural garden design
Description: [Urbana] : 3 Fields Books, an imprint of the University of Illinois Press, 2023. | Includes bibliographical references and index.
Identifiers: LCCN 2022022520 (print) | LCCN 2022022521 (ebook) | ISBN 9780252086779 (paperback) | ISBN 9780252053719 (ebook)
Subjects: LCSH: Prairie gardening—Middle West. | Landscape design—Middle West. | Endemic plants—Middle West.
Classification: LCC SB434.3.V64 2023 (print) | LCC SB434.3 (ebook) | DDC 712.0977—dc23/eng/20220722
LC record available at https://lccn.loc.gov/2022022520
LC ebook record available at https://lccn.loc.gov/2022022521

"No clipped hedges!"

—JENS JENSEN

CONTENTS

PRAIRIE UP

Canada goldenrod (*Solidago speciosa*) and big bluestem (*Andropogon gerardii*) on a restored tallgrass prairie.

1

BRINGING THE PRAIRIE HOME

"I remember coming out upon the northern Great Plains in the late spring. There were meadows of blue and yellow wildflowers on the slopes, and I could see the still, sunlit plain below reaching away out of sight. At first there is no discrimination in the eye, nothing but the land itself, whole and impenetrable. But then the smallest things begin to stand out of the depths—herds and rivers and groves—and each of these has perfect being in terms of distance and of silence and of age. Yes, I thought, now I see the earth as it really is; never again will I see things as I saw them yesterday or the day before."

—N. SCOTT MOMADAY

"The beauty and quiet calm of the grassland should not obscure the fact that the prairie is a field of battle centuries old in which the conflicting species, never wholly victorious nor entirely vanquished, each year renew the struggle. . . . Parent plants must compete with their own offspring; as a result the population becomes enormously overcrowded for the best development of the individual. Consequently all are reduced in size and underdeveloped compared to the stature they could attain. They often fruit sparingly rather than abundantly, and take years to accomplish what, unhindered by their fellows, might be accomplished in a single season."

—J. E. WEAVER

In the late afternoon of July the prairie reaches a crescendo. Under a hot sun, dry wind eases through the tallgrass while monarch and painted lady butterflies quench their thirst at a blazingstar. Bumble bee workers circle the heads of coneflowers gathering pollen. Dickcissel birds rise from the shade of bluestem and indiangrass with their eponymous dick-CISSEL-CISSEL calls. As the sun works its way farther west into evening, a coolness settles in the valleys as plants transpire, their exhalations creating a dampness that thickens the air. The quiet of this space creates a distance that can be unnerving. It is just you and the horizon, just you and the sky fading into the grass, all made part of something much larger and older than yourself.

The colors change in these golden hours as afternoon fades into evening. Bright greens are washed in faint blues, the yellow tops of coreopsis and sunflower mute to burnt orange and copper, and the purple prairie clover blooms shift to a magenta as moths take their turn to feast. Walk into a prairie at any time of day and it's like entering a Jacuzzi bath; you are delightfully vulnerable, soothed of everything you've dragged around all day, trusting in the place to hold you close, to give you back your one wild and precious life. Sit down among the plants and watch a banded orb weaver create a web larger than a cookie sheet, strung between a few blades of arching switchgrass. Prairie becomes a word synonymous with empathy and gratitude; it is not a simple place but one full of meaning that stretches out through time.

The history of my childhood, too, carries a similar weight embedded in grasslands, from the mixed grass of western Oklahoma to the savanna and forest edge of south-central Minnesota. It wasn't until I was researching for a memoir that I fully understood how my earliest days on the Plains shaped my psyche and awareness of prairie ecosystems.

My Mennonite-German great-great-grandparents made Oklahoma land runs into Cheyenne and Arapaho reservations in the 1890s to farm red winter wheat. My ancestors saw prairie, real prairie—bison herds that took days to pass and prairie dog towns that stretched to the horizon. And in a decade or two, my ancestors helped eradicate diverse, healthy ecosystems that had been as resilient and tough as the people who sailed across the Atlantic subsisting only on zwieback toast that wouldn't stay down. I come from a people whose sinew is built from the plains, but also for whom order and productivity are paramount.

I feel claustrophobic in any woodland, quickly become disoriented, and fear I'm being stalked. But put me in an open space, perhaps where I can see the long drag of dust behind an approaching car or the emerald hue of a roll cloud moving in, and I feel like a weight has been lifted off my chest. From the scrub and little bluestem in the Wichita Mountains and Gyp Hills of Oklahoma, to the reflective 10,000+ lakes surrounded by intermingling tallgrass meadows of

A windmill and small barn surrounded by winter wheat on the 1894 homestead of the author's family in Corn, Oklahoma.

Minnesota, distance is a physical and emotional force that brings me deeper into the place I and countless species call home.

It's easy to drive through a grassland and think there's nothing there—no nuance and no life. But if you stop for even a few moments to observe a single square foot, you'll find beetles walking the ground, crab spiders perched in blooms, ants farming aphids, and lacewing eggs hanging from the underside of a leaf.

Gardening from a prairie perspective means opening up our hearts and minds to these small wonders, as well as to a different method of design and management than traditional landscaping. Gardening from a prairie perspective means opening up to the perceptions and cultures of other creatures, and even other humans. Gardening from a prairie perspective means coming to terms with what we've eroded and how we can revive wildness in our communities. Ultimately, it's about the history of place and the history of close interaction, where one life depends on another for survival, even if that survival is predicated on a brutal truth—that nature is red in tooth and claw.

Plants in a prairie don't help each other so much as they jockey and tussle for survival. When one goes down, another steps in, and the competition for

Early succession plants like wild bergamot (*Monarda fistulosa*), grey-head coneflower (*Ratibida pinnata*), and hoary vervain (*Verbena stricta*) compete with big bluestem on a young meadow planting. These aggressive-seeding forb species help stabilize the soil and rebuild the plant community in the early years.

light, soil, and moisture is keen even among relatives. Often, when we bring these wild plants into a more ordered garden setting, they become so liberated that their behavior changes: stiff goldenrod doubles in height and then flops over to the ground, or ironweed self-sows in every open space until the garden is ironweed nirvana. Out in the middle of a grassland expanse, these plants share the same square foot with potentially dozens of other plant species. This competition means, for example, that stiff goldenrod may reach only 2 feet tall in the wild; yet in a pampered garden—even if it's planted thickly and layered—one can almost hear it sigh in delight as it reaches 4 feet tall. Suddenly, we have to consider cutting it back in early summer so that when it blooms in September, we aren't fussing with stakes and making gardening harder than it needs to be. Bringing the prairie home proves not to be a simple matter, and maybe that's because we first need to understand it better.

What is a prairie, a grassland, and a meadow? Where are they, and what can we learn from them as we create ecologically meaningful gardens at home and in our cities? Grasslands cover one-third of the world's landmass. The original extent of North America's Great Plains, host to some 5,000 plant species, is usually thought of as a space stretching roughly from Edmonton to Winnipeg in southern Canada, with a north-south line on its eastern edge, down through Fargo, Kansas City, slicing southwest through Tulsa and Oklahoma City, turning south toward Dallas and to the Mexican border. On the western flank, it skirts the Rockies west of Roswell, up through Denver and Casper, jutting northwest at Billings and heading north past Calgary. Other maps have a sizable bulge of tallgrass that moves east into Missouri, Iowa, Minnesota, Wisconsin, and Illinois, with fingers reaching out into Indiana, Michigan, and Ohio to create the midwestern prairies. Roughly 8,000 to 9,000 years ago, in a warmer climate, prairie species are believed to have moved east, which is why the central United States shares so many plants with Atlantic states today.

The rocky conditions of Toadstool Geological Park provide the perfect environment for dry, shortgrass meadows; sawsepal penstemon (*P. glaber*) changes bloom color based on moisture conditions.

Carizzo Plain National Monument, northwest of Los Angeles, is some 246,000 acres and features the largest remaining grassland in California. © Saxon Holt / PhotoBotanic. Used with permission.

Dotted with lakes and wetlands, the Nebraska Sandhills is a unique, mixed-grass prairie encompassing about one-quarter of the state; it is the only place where the vast underground Ogallala Aquifer (spanning from Nebraska to Texas) is recharging. The hills are the largest sand dune formation in the western hemisphere and a major migratory and breeding region for birds. © Saxon Holt / PhotoBotanic. Used with permission.

Big Meadows, near the center of Shenandoah National Park in Virginia, features wide-open spaces within the larger forests. This area has the highest concentration of rare plants in the entire park. © Paul Westervelt. Used with permission.

Coastal longleaf pine savannas are endemic to the Southeast. Big Island Prairie at Green Swamp Ecological Preserve in North Carolina represents some of the last vestiges of this once massive system that stretched from Virginia to Florida and Texas, having lost 95 percent of its historic range. © Alan Cressler. Used with permission.

Many of the most diverse Piedmont Prairie remnants can be found along power line cuts and roadsides where the landscape is managed to keep woody plants at bay. These grasslands and savannas are endemic from Virginia to Alabama. © Devin Floyd / Center for Urban Habitats. Used with permission.

Grasslands in the United States certainly aren't limited to flyover country. The Western Gulf Coast grasslands of Louisiana and Texas are composed of marshes, tallgrass prairies, and live oak woodlands. The Edwards Plateau of Texas is an ecologically unique oak woodland and mesquite savanna grassland that ranges in elevation from 100 to 3,000 feet above sea level. The Montana Valley and Foothill grasslands is a biodiverse region along the Rocky Mountain front. The Great Basin desert steppe, primarily in Nevada and Utah, includes cold-tolerant shrub species, such as sagebrushes, saltbrushes, and winterfat. The Palouse grasslands, in the rain shadow of the Cascade Mountains in Washington, Oregon, and Idaho, were once dominated by native bluebunch wheatgrass and Idaho fescue, but are now more than 99 percent converted. Formerly composed of a wide variety of perennial grasses, riparian forests, vernal pools, wetlands, chaparral shrub, and open oak savanna, less than 1 percent of pre-settlement California grasslands remain. And the Southeast is generally forgotten as a home to countless and expansive grasslands, particularly in the Piedmont region stretching from Alabama through the Carolinas into Virginia, not to mention the longleaf pine coastal savannas. In summation: prairie is everywhere.

In the central United States, the Great Plains can be broken down further: the Nebraska sandhills, the High Plains, southwestern tablelands, and the central plains. There's tallgrass, mixed grass, midgrass, shortgrass, sand prairie, cool-season mixed grass, semi-desert and steppe, saline and foothill. So many ways to describe a place even as we ultimately use one term to encapsulate it all.

When French explorers first set foot in the region, they had no word for what they saw, so they called it "prairie," their word for meadow or open glade among a wood. However, North American grasslands have less than 10 percent tree cover, and those trees tend to be in riparian areas near rivers, streams, and ponds that support most of the vertebrate species. Where trees are more numerous but still dominated by an understory of grass, we use the term savanna. A clearing of grass and flowers surrounded by woods may be called a meadow.

But for all intents and purposes, most folks use these words interchangeably—for what we have in mind is a field of grass and flowers, a field of a few thousand feet, several acres, or stretching out to the horizon. Prairie is not just a scientific or ecological term; it's an aesthetic experience that taps into our genetic memory, calling forth a primal awareness that we are safer in an open expanse where we can see dangers coming and have time to react.

In the eastern plains, 200 million acres of tallgrass once dominated, thanks in part to annual moisture totals that can reach 50", but it has lost 98 percent of its range, according to Audubon's North American Grasslands & Birds Report.

The mixed-grass region (140 million acres) has diminished by 75 percent, and the shortgrass (265 million acres)—where as little as 10" of moisture may fall in any given year—has shrunk by roughly 50 percent.

The Great Plains slope west to east at 10 feet per mile, with rivers draining toward the Mississippi, and are grass-dominated while depending on fire for rejuvenation. Some would say they also depend on grazing, since it was the massive herds of bison that created necessary disturbance by nibbling down grasses so forbs could germinate, that spread seed on their hair, that trampled said seed into the earth, and that wallowed in the dirt to create small depressions where rainwater would pool.

The natural pressures on organisms in the Plains are intense, exacerbated by the pressures of human civilization. These landscapes are rich in biodiversity. In fact, the World Wildlife Fund notes that in northern mixed prairies, the species richness index is 2,095; in contrast, highly valued landscapes like rain forests in northern California hold an index of 1,710, and the Florida Everglades 1,855 (see Candace Savage's book *Prairie*). Yet, since 1970, the northernmost ecosystems of the Great Plains have shifted 365 miles north, while the southern boundary has slid some 160 miles north, according to a University of Nebraska study led by Caleb Roberts that used bird distribution data as an indicator. The reason for this shift in geographic range isn't only climate change but also fire suppression, land use changes, and tree invasion, among other factors. Taken together, prairie is threatened if not on life support.

Larger grassland ecosystems do best with the presence of keystone species, like black-tailed prairie dogs that as many as 100 other species may depend on in some way. Prairie dog towns feature clipped foliage to better see predators, and the nutritious new growth is prized by grazers such as bison, which are also a keystone species that create necessary disturbance.

Even the dry line that separates the tallgrass and mixed grass—the 100th meridian—has moved east roughly 140 miles. This line marks a change in rainfall from 24" on its eastern edge to 18" on the west. Essentially, this means central Nebraska has moved into eastern Nebraska near the Iowa border.

As the climate changes, one oft-studied plant species signals how the environment is reacting. Big bluestem (*Andropogon gerardii*)—which grows 4–8 feet high—is predicted to reduce its stature by up to 60 percent over the next 75 years as rainfall patterns change, according to a study led by Adam Smith. Since big bluestem is a dominant species in the central and eastern plains as well as the Midwest, the ecosystem may begin to function in radically different ways. Of course, prairies are used to stress—they are built on it and thus are generally resilient and adaptable. If climate change will make the region hotter and drier, we only have to look to the not-so-distant past to see what may happen and how our landscapes—even our gardens—will shift and how we can help them become more resilient and adaptable.

This bison is feeding in the open meadows of the Wichita Mountains Wildlife Refuge in southwestern Oklahoma.

In the 1930s and '40s, famed grassland ecologist John Weaver, along with his former student F. W. Albertson, traced how thirty prairie sites in Nebraska, Iowa, Kansas, and Colorado responded to the Dust Bowl. What they saw was the massive dying out of species like big bluestem and little bluestem, replaced by prairie dropseed, porcupine grass, and especially western wheatgrass, which crowded out most other grasses in its range.

Weaver and Albertson also noted how the flower composition changed on these prairies. Forbs with bulbs and corms—which store food safely underground—expanded their ranges. So plants like violet wood-sorrel, bracted spiderwort, and wild garlic did well. Additional forbs that proliferated included prairie ragwort, white sage, and yarrow. In fact, heath aster did so well that Weaver and Albertson were dismayed to find it covering entire fields—since its forage value is so low, they grimaced at its expansiveness even as they grudgingly remarked it covered the ground and held soil in place. Because grasslands depend on disturbance, such as fire and grazing, they also may depend on fluctuating climate patterns, such as drought. Drought is almost a predictable occurrence, as major drought years have shown (1870, 1892–96,

A restored prairie on a rural acreage was created almost entirely from seed. Over the course of a decade, the forbs and grasses have self-organized, coming and going in various years as changing weather and management create new opportunities.

1930s, 1950s, 1970s, 1999–2006). For plant and animal diversity to continue through time, communities must ebb and flow, diminish and proliferate; it's a hard but important lesson as we consider how best to design and manage natural gardens and what plants we make sure to include.

For example, the benefits of grasses are numerous and critical to a thriving ecosystem, as we'll see when we come to garden design and management in future chapters. Let's compare one acre of Wisconsin timberland to one acre of tallgrass: in the former, 90 tons of plant mass lies above the soil, with another 80 tons of organic material in the top 42" of the soil. A tallgrass prairie has only 3 tons of plant material out in the open but some 150 tons of organic material in the top 42" of soil. This is why, at one point, 18" of rich, fertile soil had accumulated, making the tallgrass region the eventual "bread basket" of the world. With 25 miles of roots in just one square yard of a big bluestem patch, it's no wonder that, as old roots decayed and new ones tunneled through and aerated the soil, the earth became more capable of supporting life. For example, in western Iowa, big bluestem may contribute 500 pounds of organic material per acre just in the top 6" of soil, and over the course of a year, decaying roots and surface leaf litter can add 900 lb. of organic material per acre.

The addition of organic material helps make prairie ecosystems self-supporting—at least in an idealized wild setting devoid of direct human influence. But even without our direct influence of plowing up prairie for new farmland or paving over the expanding edges of cities, our indirect influence is pronounced. We have already surpassed 415 ppm of CO_2 in the atmosphere, and this will fundamentally alter plants in profound ways. For example, a study led by Ellen Welti at the Konza Prairie Biological Station in northeastern Kansas notes that grasshoppers are on the decline, and the main reason might be nutrient loss in plants.

The study traces 44 grasshopper species, using data from two studies, one spanning from 1996 to 2017 in an undisturbed prairie and another from 2002 to 2017 where bison graze regularly. Grasshoppers declined 30 percent in those two decades, and habitat loss and pesticides aren't factors in this intact ecosystem. The authors believe that increasing atmospheric CO_2 is leading to a loss of nitrogen, phosphorus, zinc, and other nutrients in plant leaves. The idea is that roots can't keep up with the carbon-stimulated extra growth above ground and so, in essence, nutrients are being diluted. Over 30 years, plant biomass on the prairies doubled, but nitrogen content dipped by 42 percent, phosphorus by 58 percent, and potassium by 54 percent.

While grasses and other plants may be losing essential nutrients for wildlife, grasses are resilient organisms in times of high heat and drought. In fact, one could say the way they function is pretty amazing. Plants take in water through roots and lose it as water vapor in their leaves through valves called stomata. The bigger the leaf, the more stomata, so smaller leaves are one adaptation grasses have made to reduce water loss. Grass leaves are also ridged or covered in hairs so it's harder for wind to whisk away moisture.

But here's where grasses get really interesting (as an ecosystem gardener, you should be nodding your head enthusiastically): on most plants, the stomata remain open so plants can breathe, and this breathing takes in CO_2, which, in combination with absorbing solar energy and mixing it with water, produces sugars and other molecules for plant growth. That's photosynthesis. But grasses schedule when their stomata open and close. At midday, their stomata close to reduce water loss while the leaf stores solar energy, and then in the evening, those stomata open up to produce the food plants need, a process that can happen even in the middle of the night.

Over several million years in Earth's history, CO_2 began to drop, which meant grass species had to evolve or perish. The older C3 grasses (cool-season grasses), which link carbon atoms to three-atom molecules, began to wit-

Little bluestem (*Schizachyrium scoparium*) provides bluish-green foliage all summer long, and then in late summer, glittery seed heads appear, followed by fall colors of copper. It's a soil-building workhorse and is found in almost every U.S. state.

A mix of various short grasses provides the core design element of this New Mexico garden, joined by native sagebrush. Grasses are an important aesthetic and ecological component of healthy gardens. © Hunter Ten Broeck. Used with permission.

ness the rise of C4 grasses (warm-season grasses). However, these new plants needed warmer temperatures (75–85°F versus 65–75°F), temperatures which helped produce a special growth enzyme.

C4 grasses are often called warm-season grasses, and they are more prevalent the farther south one goes. C3 grasses are cool season and are more numerous farther north. Of course, both grasses grow fine together, because C3 grasses leap out primarily in spring and set seed by early summer, while C4 grasses don't really get going until late spring and early summer, setting seed in late summer and early fall. The two kinds of grass fill niches, using water and sunlight at different times of the year, yet when growing together, they keep the ground covered and provide all the ecosystem benefits grasses create, from soil stabilization to weed control. This may be our first important lesson about natural garden design—using plants to fill environmental niches.

As we enter the great uncertainty of human-caused climate change, grasslands and biodiverse pocket prairies in urban areas will be critical in mitigating some of the negative effects. Over larger expanses, grasslands are more reliable carbon sinks than forests because most carbon is stored underground and won't be released when fires move through; they are also some of the most cost-effective and scalable ecosystems to sequester carbon. Simply slowing grassland conversion to croplands would mitigate the loss of 28 percent of the carbon stored in soil, while the sequestration rates of CO_2 are best in the Midwest, northern Plains, and Southeast. Employing not only cover crops but also strategically placed prairie strips (10 percent of total acreage) in agricultural fields will help increase sequestration and, in the case of prairie strips, reduce topsoil loss by 95 percent and fertilizer runoff by 84–90 percent. Another benefit is supporting beneficial predator bugs and insects that can lessen the reliance on pesticides while creating habitat corridors for wildlife.

Showy goldenrod (*Solidago speciosa*) punctuates the semi-urban entrance to the University of Wisconsin Madison Arboretum's visitor center, which is adjacent to the oldest restored prairie in the lower 48 states.

We can create similar benefits in areas where we live and work, in urban and suburban locations, realizing that prairie plants employed within their natural plant communities can guide us as we create beautiful, resilient gardens that benefit all species together. But maybe you're asking why all this prairie exploration matters when smaller gardens are so different? They are so much smaller and can't ever hope to act like a real prairie. But what prairies teach us is profound scientifically, ecologically, and even emotionally and psychologically. The success of a garden isn't just about plants staying alive and looking good, but also doing good. Plants aren't just decorations.

All plants sequester carbon while helping rainfall penetrate deep into soil and holding on to that rainfall with their leaves, so less water hits the ground, which reduces flash flooding. In an urban environment, a plant's ability to clean the air and reduce flooding is critical (more on this in chapter 2). But plants also cool the air via transpiration and shading. And plants support people's health

A median planting on a busy Denver thoroughfare highlights a mostly native palette suitable for the ecoregion and harsh roadside conditions. © Graham Gardner. Used with permission.

The same planting in autumn, which exemplifies how beauty and ecosystem function continue through all seasons. © Graham Gardner. Used with permission.

The Chelsea Grasslands on the High Line in New York City shows what's possible where we most need the ecosystem services of lush, natural plantings. © Les Parks. Used with permission.

Even small areas in confined spaces—like this elevated rooftop bed at the Monona Terrace Community and Convention Center in Madison, Wisconsin—can have designed, resilient native plant communities. Some of these plants might be good options for apartment deck planters. © Tony Gomez-Phillips. Used with permission.

A pocket prairie outside an office building serves as a habitat waystation while reducing management costs.

and well-being through these mechanisms, as well as through creating the type of environment that reduces allergies.

In urban and even rural areas, the lack of native plant communities may actually increase the occurrence of allergies in people. In a study led by Ilkka Hanski in Finland, teenagers were observed to have lower allergy rates when they were exposed to certain bacteria on their skin that are common in native plant communities. The loss of such biodiversity around homes and schools may actually harm us. This study predicts that by 2050, two-thirds of humanity will live in areas with limited contact with nature, while an increasing number of people will suffer from chronic inflammatory disorders, including allergies and autoimmune diseases. The more contact we have with nature, the more we come in contact with microbiota that stimulate our immune responses early in life, thus protecting us down the road.

If we look toward the prairie as a guide, we find a wealth of knowledge we've forgotten or never knew—yet it's also a wealth our bodies know deeply. In the preservation of nature is the preservation of ourselves, and for many of us, the act of gardening provides the most intimate terms for cultivating preservation, community, and understanding of all we depend on.

I think of conservationist Aldo Leopold in *A Sand County Almanac* lamenting a compass plant in an old pioneer prairie in late July, and I find his words most fitting for the work we have at hand as gardeners of small and large landscapes across the world: "Heretofore unreachable by scythe or mower, this yard-square relic of original Wisconsin gives birth, each July, to a man-high stalk of compass plant or cutleaf Silphium, spangled with saucer-sized yellow blooms resembling sunflowers. It is the sole remnant of this plant along this highway, and perhaps the sole remnant in the western half of our county. What a thousand acres of Silphiums looked like when they tickled the bellies of the buffalo is a question never again to be answered, and perhaps not even asked."

Urban and suburban landscapes of all sizes are rife with opportunity to rethink how we use outdoor spaces, like this living lab for college students. © Tyler Moore. Used with permission.

The next week, Leopold returned to check on his friend, only to find it mowed down with the rest of the remnant prairie plants. He said:

> It is easy now to predict the future; for a few years my Silphium will try in vain to rise above the mowing machine, and then it will die. With it will die the prairie epoch. The Highway Department says that 100,000 cars pass yearly over this route during the three summer months when the Silphium is in bloom. In them must ride at least 100,000 people who have "taken" what is called history, and perhaps 25,000 who have "taken" what is called botany. Yet I doubt whether a dozen have seen the Silphium, and of these hardly one will notice its demise. If I were to tell a preacher of the adjoining church that the road crew has been burning history books in his cemetery, under the guise of mowing weeds, he would be amazed and uncomprehending. How could a weed be a book?

It is time for us to artfully cultivate weeds and add a radical new chapter to the history of grasslands and human disturbance. It is time to bring the prairie home.

Masses and drifts of forbs mix naturally with grasses to form a thriving ecological community in a backyard landscape. © Austin Eischeid Garden Design and Jensen Ecology. Used with permission.

2

LEARNING ABOUT NATIVE PLANTS AND PLANT COMMUNITIES

"There might be as many as thirty million species of insects . . . rapidly disappearing. The current extinction rate is four hundred times that of the recent geologic past and climbing. It is an odd irony that the places we call empty should retain some memory of the diversity of life, while the places we have filled up grow emptier and emptier."
—PAUL GRUCHOW

You'll be hard-pressed to find virgin prairie in urban and suburban areas, although a few spots exist. It's not just a sad travesty that gets us in the gut, or an indictment, or even a call to action—the fact is it's all those things together, as well as a real threat to our community health and infrastructure.

Even if we restored habitat patches in the urban and rural edge environment, we'd still have only a fraction of the ecosystem function, as well as only a fraction of the needed landmass. In a study that looked at more than 3,000 restored ecosystems after 150 years, these ecosystems had 30 percent less diversity and 40 percent less function than an undisturbed habitat (see lecture by David Mateos). Basically, between nutrient exchanges and soil life, there's just too much complexity we can't easily revive or replicate, which means it's paramount that we first conserve and revive what's left of wilder areas. If our designed gardens are intended to be habitat for fauna, we're going to have to

A female long-horned bee specialist (*Melissodes*) gathers pollen on a sneezeweed (*Helenium autumnale*).

Viceroys look a lot like monarchs, but their host plants include willows (*Salix* spp.), poplars, and cottonwoods (*Populus* spp.). Here, an adult fuels up on New England aster (*Symphyotrichum novae-angliae*).

learn not only how those fauna fare in highly altered landscapes but also how they use the plants found there.

In more urban or built areas, helping wildlife comes with the caveat that such areas increase pressures on pollinating insect species. Although these insects' ability to forage tends to improve because these areas contain more flowers than monoculture-dominated rural areas do, as urbanization increases, the sex of bees becomes more male-dominated. Since male and female bees tend to pollinate different plant species, this shift can affect plant reproduction and diversity, which in turn affects pollen and nectar available for a wide range of pollinators.

Black swallowtail larvae feed on native and exotic plants in the carrot family, including golden Alexanders (*Zizia aurea*) and fennel (*Foeniculum vulgare*).

Large milkweed bugs (*Oncopeltus fasciatus*) are just one of many species that use milkweed (*Asclepias* spp.) as a host plant, eating the seed in late summer and autumn before migrating south.

All that being said, bumble bees tend to have higher reproduction rates in cities than in rural areas, but as the urban heat island effect intensifies, every 1°C increase of temperature reduces wild bee populations by 40 percent, according to a study led by April Hamblin. One related study led by Kris Sales suggests that a five-day heat wave can decrease male beetle fertility by as much as 75 percent. According to another study led by Matthew Forister that casts a wider net, a 3.2°C global increase, predicted by the end of the century or sooner, will see 50 percent of all insects having their ranges reduced by half. But if we can limit the increase to 2°C, only 18 percent of insects will be so affected.

One further pressure on urban pollinators in our gardens includes light pollution, which can help predators see insects, attract moths to their deaths, and obscure mating signals, as is the case with fireflies. Blue light emitted by LED streetlights can also affect the circadian rhythm of both insects and other species, complicating forage, sleep, and reproductive patterns. One study led by Avalon Owens suggested that 100 billion insects die annually in Germany alone because of attraction to car headlights.

THE IMPORTANCE OF SPECIALIST BEES

As many as 25 percent of bee species in any particular region are specialists, and more than 3,700 native bee species exist in the United States alone. The presence of specialist bees increases plant diversity, ecosystem function, and even pollination of some food crops, because they show floral fidelity, focusing on one or several species for efficient pollen spread as they visit blooms. Yet because specialist bees forage on a limited group of plants, this creates a precarious scenario–especially given the pressure of human development and climate disruption. As bloom periods go out of sync with bee emergence, and because many bees have timed their limited lifespan (often just a few weeks) to coincide with their preferred flower, bees and the plants themselves may struggle as the landscape is altered. Here's an introductory fact list on these important insects:

- Oligolectic bees specialize on the pollen of one plant family.
- Monolectic bees specialize on the pollen of one plant genus.
- Specialist bees improve plant pollination through floral fidelity.
- Improved pollination (floral fidelity) increases host plant abundance.
- The Asteraceae family is the most supportive group of plants.
- Trees and shrubs also host specialist bees, including willow (*Salix* spp.), which may support dozens of species in some regions.
- Native plants that provide pollen for specialist bees also support the larvae of specialist butterflies and moths.

If we're going to rethink pretty in our gardens—if we're going to value ecosystem function as much as aesthetics—we have to shift our concept of function. Looking across a rolling prairie, we generally find it beautiful, and we know it's probably doing a lot of environmental good, compared with a monoculture of soybeans or lawn. Yet, if you put even an echo of that landscape into a more urban area, suddenly it's wild, messy, and attractive to pests—or so the traditional line of thinking goes. There may be an issue of scale here—when wildness is confined, especially within the hard rectilinear angles of human development, said wildness is amplified, so even an echo of wildness may be threatening to our animal instincts of survival from dangers large and small that lurk in the shadows. A middle ground exists, though, and one path is to advocate for plants' usefulness—not only to provide beauty for us or food for pollinators, but also as part of a community infrastructure that improves our health and reduces costs, from water treatment (soaking up heavy rains) to energy use (shading structures) and health care (plants purify the air).

One way plants are useful that home gardeners may overlook is phytoremediation, or a plant's ability to clean the environment. We know that plants can reduce storm runoff by both absorbing rainfall in their root systems and holding on to it via their leaves and branches. And yet we can also use plants to clean contaminated soil and water while rebuilding the soil's biologic community. Some high-biomass plants are reliable performers in phytoremediation, including switchgrass (*Panicum* spp.) and willow (*Salix* spp.). Some species also have a high evapotranspiration rate, which is the process of moving water from the soil to the air, and this process can better capture and filter out contaminants. The best tree species for high evapotranspiration to clean soil and groundwater include river birch, ash, cottonwood, mesquite, aspen, and bald cypress.

Generally, if a site is known to be contaminated by petroleum products, which are common in human environments, you'll want 10 lb. of grass seed per acre or one tree per 75 square feet. Organic compounds—such as petroleum, atrazine, volatile organic compounds (VOCs), and chlorinated solvents (think dry cleaners)—are easier to break down, taking 1–10 years, while heavy metals may take decades.

Some of the best native grasses to work on petroleum-contaminated soil include big bluestem, indiangrass, switchgrass, sideoats grama, blue grama, canada wild rye, and bottlebrush grass. For woody natives, the list expands to hackberry, honeylocust, redbud, loblolly

Suburban landscapes hold great promise for the rejuvenation of biodiversity and the health of all species when they take their inspiration from natural plant communities.

The ecosystem services that backyard gardens provide can be extensive, no matter their size. Island beds can slow storm runoff, naturally amend soil, and increase habitat for wildlife, all while looking intentional. © Kevin O'Brien. Used with permission.

Masses and drifts of flowers emerge from side-oats grama (*Bouteloua curtipendula*). The environmental benefit of this acreage border is exponentially larger than that of a lawn monoculture.

This garden was originally planted to soak up standing water that gathered not only from a slight slope but also from the lot next door. Water that stood inches deep for a day is now gone within hours.

pine, bur oak, and black willow. And for forbs, we can include sunflowers, goldenrods, and legumes (such as prairie clover, lead plant, and false indigo). Ultimately, when we plan our gardens, the way we think of plants can affect not only how we design but also how we value and experience the design. When we combine plants' aesthetic and practical usefulness, suddenly a garden of any size on any site becomes an entry point into seeing plants as critical to our future, our health, and our safety.

I remember the first time I experienced queen of the prairie (*Filipendula rubra*) in bloom, which was at a mom-and-pop nursery—the now-defunct Ambergate Gardens. I'd never seen anything like this plant: an airy cloud of pink flowers reminiscent of cotton candy mating with a thick puff of breath in wintertime. It didn't look like any prairie plant I'd ever seen, and its profound

While the majority of this sown garden is allowed to discover its own way, other portions are more intentionally planted and maintained, like a seating area featuring semi-formal conifers and other non-prairie selections at the bottom of the steps. This juxtaposition can provide environmental benefits, such as increasing edge habitat, while allowing the gardener to satisfy various design urges.

fragrance echoed of roses. I read the tag, did some whirlwind internet research, and before long, I had it in my collection near a downspout—a solitary plant surrounded by wood mulch. After a few years, it began to spread underground until a nearby river birch shaded it into oblivion. I still walk by the spot where a few stalks, only several inches tall, try to get going in spring, but I miss the flowers for the excitement they once brought me as a new gardener discovering plants for the first time.

How do we choose plants for our gardens? Do we walk into a nursery hoping to discover something new that delights our senses, or do we explore a nearby natural area and wonder how it works? What if I told you that doing both might be the key to creating the kind of garden that best melds the aesthetic and environmental expectations we have for our home landscapes?

TAXONOMIC CLASSIFICATION

Learning about plants means being able to discuss them accurately using binomial nomenclature or scientific names. The most you're likely ever going to need are family, genus, and species. As an example, here's what purple coneflower looks like:

Domain–Eukaryota
Kingdom–Plantae
Phylum–Spermatophyta
Class–Dicotyledonae
Order–Asterales
Family–Asteraceae
Genus–Echinacea
Species–Purpurea

At the nursery, the primary way we're going to know if a plant is right for us is by looking at the plant tag, a small sliver of information that lists a vague set of parameters that may or may not apply to where we live. In general, the label will have the following information:

Common name
Scientific name
USDA hardiness zone
Bloom time
Size
Sun and drainage requirements

It may shock you, but that's not enough information–and it may be the wrong information. An Echinacea species that is native to both Ohio and Arkansas is going to perform differently, from bloom time to mature size–all features that will be affected by factors such as varied site conditions, ranging from soil type to plant competition to microclimates around your house. And "well-drained soil" on a plant tag could mean sand, loam, gravel, or something in between; that's a lot of ground to cover (pun intended) that is critical to know if you want plants to thrive. So how can you go a step further and create a more accurate list of information? By looking at the following:

Ecoregion–the local geographical community and conditions
Seasonal habit–how it performs in all four seasons
Lifespan–long- or short-lived, and in what site conditions
Root zone–fibrous, taproot, corm, bulb
Method of reproduction–clumper, seed, runner
Garden management–thinning, replanting, overseeding, when to cut back
Wildlife support–adult insects, larval insects and bugs, birds

Let's explore some of the above parameters in more detail and learn where you can find information to make appropriate plant decisions, as well as how to know your home ground better.

Ecoregion

We're accustomed to choosing plants by U.S. Department of Agriculture (USDA) hardiness zone, which is a measure of minimum cold temperatures in winter that a plant can usually survive. Hardiness zones are shifting north and uphill as the climate warms, and about every ten years these maps are updated. Further complicating hardiness zones are broad differences among regions, despite their being categorized within the same zone. For example, zone 5 in New York State is not the same as zone 5 in Colorado, particularly when working with native plants. The two regions are vastly different, from climate to plant communities, not to mention other factors in ecosystem function, such as wildlife support.

WHAT IS LOCAL ECOTYPE?

While a plant species may be native across a large area of the United States, genetic variations influence how a plant grows in specific ecoregions. Using local ecotype seed, or plants grown from local ecotype seed, gives those species the best chance to thrive in the immediate environment, from disease resilience to reproduction to bloom times in sync with pollinators. Local ecotype range is defined differently depending on what organization you're talking to, and it can vary from as little as a few miles to 50 or 100 miles. Using local ecotype seed is critical for restoration work, even if it's harder to come by and / or more expensive. For home gardeners not adjacent to undisturbed areas, it's not always as important.

A more accurate way to begin your native plant search is to look at ecoregion maps, compiled by the U.S. Environmental Protection Agency (EPA). You'll find four versions of these maps, from level 1, which shows 15 broad ecoregions, to level 4, which highlights 967. For most gardeners, it's probably best to work with either level 2 (25 regions) or level 3 (105 regions), depending on how local you want to go with your plant selection and matching to your site. For example, ecoregions are super handy for conservationists needing to learn about a site to conserve or revive the landscape.

Why do ecoregions matter? Because they aren't looking at just cold hardiness but also other critical aspects, such as geology, soils, climate, hydrology, wildlife, and plant communities. If one of our goals is to garden for wildlife, choosing plants endemic to a specific ecoregion will help fine-tune landscapes

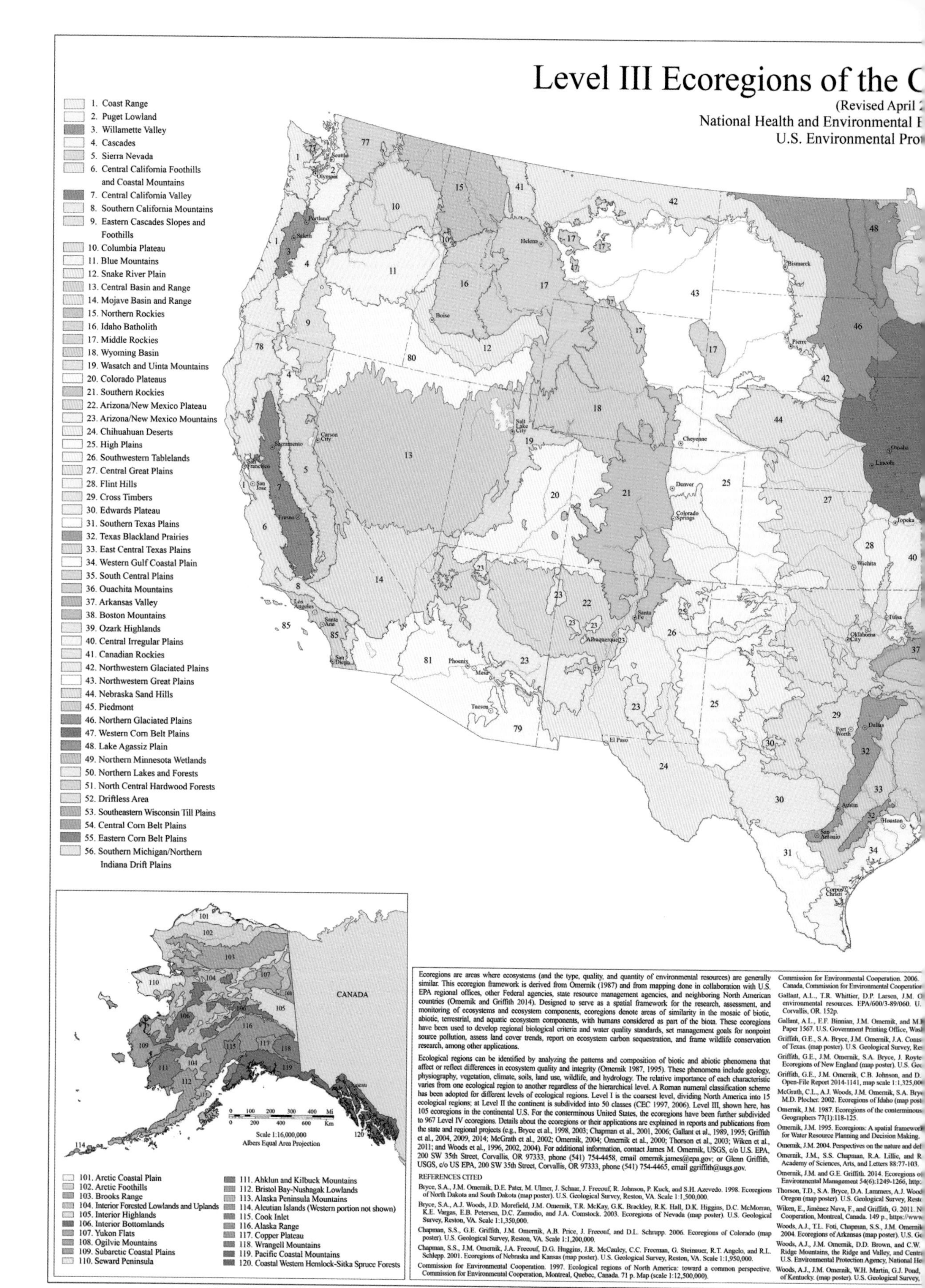

Level III Ecoregions of the
(Revised April
National Health and Environmental
U.S. Environmental
1. Coast Range
2. Puget Lowland
3. Willamette Valley
4. Cascades
5. Sierra Nevada
6. Central California Foothills and Coastal Mountains
7. Central California Valley
8. Southern California Mountains
9. Eastern Cascades Slopes and Foothills
10. Columbia Plateau
11. Blue Mountains
12. Snake River Plain
13. Central Basin and Range
14. Mojave Basin and Range
15. Northern Rockies
16. Idaho Batholith
17. Middle Rockies
18. Wyoming Basin
19. Wasatch and Uinta Mountains
20. Colorado Plateaus
21. Southern Rockies
22. Arizona/New Mexico Plateau
23. Arizona/New Mexico Mountains
24. Chihuahuan Deserts
25. High Plains
26. Southwestern Tablelands
27. Central Great Plains
28. Flint Hills
29. Cross Timbers
30. Edwards Plateau
31. Southern Texas Plains
32. Texas Blackland Prairies
33. East Central Texas Plains
34. Western Gulf Coastal Plain
35. South Central Plains
36. Ouachita Mountains
37. Arkansas Valley
38. Boston Mountains
39. Ozark Highlands
40. Central Irregular Plains
41. Canadian Rockies
42. Northwestern Glaciated Plains
43. Northwestern Great Plains
44. Nebraska Sand Hills
45. Piedmont
46. Northern Glaciated Plains
47. Western Corn Belt Plains
48. Lake Agassiz Plain
49. Northern Minnesota Wetlands
50. Northern Lakes and Forests
51. North Central Hardwood Forests
52. Driftless Area
53. Southeastern Wisconsin Till Plains
54. Central Corn Belt Plains
55. Eastern Corn Belt Plains
56. Southern Michigan/Northern Indiana Drift Plains
Seattle
Olympia
Portland
Salem
Helena
Bismarck
Boise
Pierre
Salt Lake City
Carson City
Sacramento
San Francisco
San Jose
Fresno
Cheyenne
Denver
Colorado Springs
Omaha
Lincoln
Topeka
Wichita
Santa Fe
Albuquerque
Los Angeles
Santa Ana
San Diego
Tulsa
Oklahoma City
Phoenix
Mesa
Tucson
El Paso
Fort Worth
Dallas
Austin
San Antonio
Houston
Corpus Christi
CANADA
0 100 200 300 400 Mi
0 200 400 600 Km
Scale 1:16,000,000
Albers Equal Area Projection
101. Arctic Coastal Plain
102. Arctic Foothills
103. Brooks Range
104. Interior Forested Lowlands and Uplands
105. Interior Highlands
106. Interior Bottomlands
107. Yukon Flats
108. Ogilvie Mountains
109. Subarctic Coastal Plains
110. Seward Peninsula
111. Ahklun and Kilbuck Mountains
112. Bristol Bay-Nushagak Lowlands
113. Alaska Peninsula Mountains
114. Aleutian Islands (Western portion not shown)
115. Cook Inlet
116. Alaska Range
117. Copper Plateau
118. Wrangell Mountains
119. Pacific Coastal Mountains
120. Coastal Western Hemlock-Sitka Spruce Forests
Ecoregions are areas where ecosystems (and the type, quality, and quantity of environmental resources) are generally similar. This ecoregion framework is derived from Omernik (1987) and from mapping done in collaboration with U.S. EPA regional offices, other Federal agencies, state resource management agencies, and neighboring North American countries (Omernik and Griffith 2014). Designed to serve as a spatial framework for the research, assessment, and monitoring of ecosystems and ecosystem components, ecoregions denote areas of similarity in the mosaic of biotic, abiotic, terrestrial, and aquatic ecosystem components, with humans considered as part of the biota. These ecoregions have been used to develop regional biological criteria and water quality standards, set management goals for nonpoint source pollution, assess land cover trends, report on ecosystem carbon sequestration, and frame wildlife conservation research, among other applications.
Ecological regions can be identified by analyzing the patterns and composition of biotic and abiotic phenomena that affect or reflect differences in ecosystem quality and integrity (Omernik 1987, 1995). These phenomena include geology, physiography, vegetation, climate, soils, land use, wildlife, and hydrology. The relative importance of each characteristic varies from one ecological region to another regardless of the hierarchical level. A Roman numeral classification scheme has been adopted for different levels of ecological regions. Level I is the coarsest level, dividing North America into 15 ecological regions; at Level II the continent is subdivided into 50 classes (CEC 1997, 2006). Level III, shown here, has 105 ecoregions in the continental U.S. For the conterminous United States, the ecoregions have been further subdivided to 967 Level IV ecoregions. Details about the ecoregions or their applications are explained in reports and publications from the state and regional projects (e.g., Bryce et al., 1998, 2003; Chapman et al., 2001, 2006; Gallant et al., 1989, 1995; Griffith et al., 2004, 2009, 2014; McGrath et al., 2002; Omernik, 2004; Omernik et al., 2000; Thorson et al., 2003; Wiken et al., 2011; and Woods et al., 1996, 2002, 2004). For additional information, contact James M. Omernik, USGS, c/o U.S. EPA, 200 SW 35th Street, Corvallis, OR 97333, phone (541) 754-4458, email omernik.james@epa.gov; or Glenn Griffith, USGS, c/o US EPA, 200 SW 35th Street, Corvallis, OR 97333, phone (541) 754-4465, email ggriffith@usgs.gov.
REFERENCES CITED
Bryce, S.A., J.M. Omernik, D.E. Pater, M. Ulmer, J. Schaar, J. Freeouf, R. Johnson, P. Kuck, and S.H. Azevedo. 1998. Ecoregions of North Dakota and South Dakota (map poster). U.S. Geological Survey, Reston, VA. Scale 1:1,500,000.
Bryce, S.A., A.J. Woods, J.D. Morefield, J.M. Omernik, T.R. McKay, G.K. Brackley, R.K. Hall, D.K. Higgins, D.C. McMorran, K.E. Vargas, E.B. Petersen, D.C. Zamudio, and J.A. Comstock. 2003. Ecoregions of Nevada (map poster). U.S. Geological Survey, Reston, VA. Scale 1:1,350,000.
Chapman, S.S., G.E. Griffith, J.M. Omernik, A.B. Price, J. Freeouf, and D.L. Schrupp. 2006. Ecoregions of Colorado (map poster). U.S. Geological Survey, Reston, VA. Scale 1:1,200,000.
Chapman, S.S., J.M. Omernik, J.A. Freeouf, D.G. Huggins, J.R. McCauley, C.C. Freeman, G. Steinauer, R.T. Angelo, and R.L. Schlepp. 2001. Ecoregions of Nebraska and Kansas (map poster). U.S. Geological Survey, Reston, VA. Scale 1:1,950,000.
Commission for Environmental Cooperation. 1997. Ecological regions of North America: toward a common perspective. Commission for Environmental Cooperation, Montreal, Quebec, Canada. 71 p. Map (scale 1:12,500,000).
Commission for Environmental Cooperation. 2006.
Canada, Commission for Environmental
Gallant, A.L., T.R. Whittier, D.P. Larsen, J.M.
environmental resources. EPA/600/3-89/060.
Corvallis, OR. 152p.
Gallant, A.L., E.F. Binnian, J.M. Omernik, and
Paper 1567. U.S. Government Printing Office,
Griffith, G.E., S.A. Bryce, J.M. Omernik, J.A.
of Texas. (map poster). U.S. Geological Survey,
Griffith, G.E., J.M. Omernik, S.A. Bryce, J.
Ecoregions of New England (map poster). U.S.
Griffith, G.E., J.M. Omernik, C.B. Johnson, and D.
Open-File Report 2014-1141, map scale
McGrath, C.L., A.J. Woods, J.M. Omernik, S.A.
M.D. Plocher. 2002. Ecoregions of Idaho (map
Omernik, J.M. 1987. Ecoregions of the conterminous
Geographers 77(1):118-125.
Omernik, J.M. 1995. Ecoregions: A spatial
for Water Resource Planning and Decision Making.
Omernik, J.M. 2004. Perspectives on the nature and
Omernik, J.M., S.S. Chapman, R.A. Lillie, and
Academy of Sciences, Arts, and Letters 88:77-103.
Omernik, J.M. and G.E. Griffith. 2014. Ecoregions
Environmental Management 54(6):1249-1266,
Thorson, T.D., S.A. Bryce, D.A. Lammers, A.J.
Oregon (map poster). U.S. Geological Survey,
Wiken, E., Jiménez Nava, F., and Griffith, G. 2011.
Cooperation, Montreal, Canada. 149 p.,
Woods, A.J., T.L. Foti, Chapman, S.S., J.M.
2004. Ecoregions of Arkansas (map poster). U.S.
Woods, A.J., J.M. Omernik, D.D. Brown, and C.W.
Ridge Mountains, the Ridge and Valley, and
U.S. Environmental Protection Agency, National
Woods, A.J., J.M. Omernik, W.H. Martin, G.J. Pond,
of Kentucky. (map poster). U.S. Geological Survey,

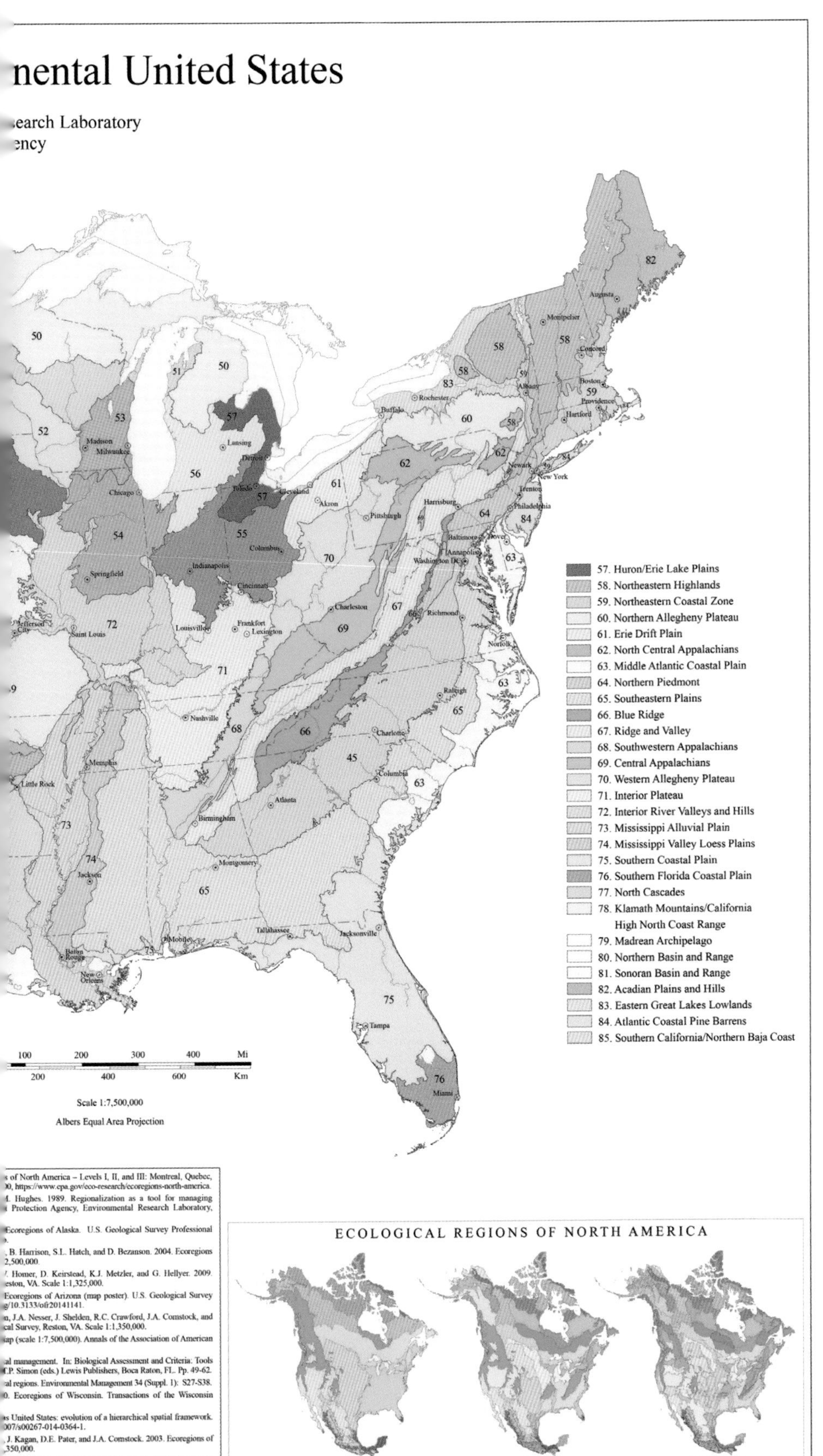

Level III ecoregion map as defined by the EPA. This is probably the most practical map for home gardeners to use when searching for native plants and working with local plant communities.

Using native plants is not limiting in a design, especially when we're landscaping for regional ecosystems. In fact, this garden goes a step further and uses only local ecotype plants. In bloom are: *Monarda fistulosa*, *Echinacea pallida*, *Echinacea purpurea*, and *Parthenium integrifolium*. © Austin Eischeid Garden Design and Jensen Ecology. Used with permission.

for that goal, especially if we're hoping to match bloom period to pollinators that time their life cycles around specific flower availability. But we're also choosing plants for suitability and adaptability, as well as what other plants will thrive alongside them, which can create a more sustainable space over time for you and for wildlife.

ON CULTIVARS

A native plant cultivar is generally either a lab-bred hybrid (a horticulturist crossed two plants for specific desirable traits) or a wild / garden hybrid or variety discovered and propagated for its unique traits. The former will read something like *Echinacea x* 'Cheyenne Spirit' and the latter *Symphyotrichum novae-angliae* 'Purple Dome,' or even *Solidago* 'Wichita Mountains,' which was discovered in Oklahoma and whose species is unknown, yet it is ubiquitous in nurseries.

At issue is whether cultivars are as supportive of larvae and adult pollinators as the straight species, which themselves are highly diverse based on ecoregion. Preliminary studies show that it depends. In general, altering height seems to have little effect on plant usage, but circumstances change when leaf color, bloom color, and flower arrangement shift.

A double-flowered *Echinacea* hybrid, which provides almost no benefit for adult pollinators.

Plants selected for purple and red leaves have increased levels of anthocyanin pigments, which deter insect larvae from eating the leaves. Plants with double flowers that conceal or are devoid of nectar and pollen are useless for adult pollinators, while a change in bloom color may alter UV markings that plants use to communicate with pollinators. Alterations of plants also may affect the nutritional quality of pollen and nectar, not to mention bloom sync with specialist pollinators.

Regardless, one of the significant issues with cultivars is that many are clones, often propagated by methods such as tissue cuttings to ensure desired traits are maintained, which means literally the same plant is sold around the country. These clones cause a lack of genetic diversity and potential loss of resilience in the face of disease or herbivory, and when planted near wild populations of the straight species, these clones may pollute the wild populations.

In the end, much research is needed on each cultivar in each ecoregion, which likely will never occur due to the great expense. It's up to gardeners and landscapers to weigh the pros and cons—the aesthetic delight of a new form and the ecosystem function of the plant choices.

For more information, you may wish to read the research conducted by Dr. Annie White, studies by Doug Tallamy, and plant trials performed by the Mt. Cuba Center.

Choosing Plants Based on Diversity

What does diversity mean? This is where we need to be aware of how garden designers and ecologists often use the term—there's much nuance to the subject, and we're still learning. For designers, diversity is usually about creating a rich aesthetic show, and for ecologists, wildlife support and ecological resilience come first. For nature-based gardeners and designers, the distinctions blur as they chart a path somewhere down the middle between aesthetics and ecosystem function.

When gardens are densely organized with a diversity of layers and plants, natural processes can get to work sooner, such as succession and climate adaptability. © Austin Eischeid Garden Design and Jensen Ecology. Used with permission.

What do we really mean when we say "diversity"? It's more than welcoming in every plant that plays well together and thrives on site, even if they all come from similar prairie or grassland ecosystems the world over. Diversity means genetic diversity, particularity of plants that support the full range of local ecosystem function. The only way a plant can move is by reproduction, which most often is seeding. Since plants are stuck in the ground, they depend on adaptability, which means they depend on producing novel mutations in their genetic code that, over time, allow the species to adapt. The more novel mutations—the more young that are different from the parent—the better, even as natural selection forces most of those variations to die out. (Of course, we select and breed many of these mutations as cultivars.) However, in a rapidly changing climate with wild swings in weather, disease, and pests, adaptation takes on even more importance.

A 2020 study by Matthew Koski showed that as the global climate warms and ozone levels decline, some plants are altering their petals to compensate. Specifically, flowers that have pollen exposed to direct sunlight are increasing petal pigmentation that absorbs harmful UV light, so the flowers are getting darker. But such pigmentation has declined in flower petals that shield pollen, primarily as a way to reduce heat that would otherwise cook the pollen. Between 1941 and 2017, flowers increased UV-absorbing pigmentation by 2 percent annually. The implication here is that a change in UV markings on petals may affect how pollinators interact with flowers, since groups like bees read those markings as runway lights to rewards or the status of nectar availability and quality.

When we think of plant diversity in gardens, the issue isn't limited to plant genetics; another way landscapes can be resilient and maintain ecological function is to create diversity of size and age. So perhaps the landscape includes a mix of young and old plants of the same species, or one part of the landscape has been replanted or intentionally disturbed (through fire, mowing, or thinning) to allow for habitat and plant variation, while another part of the landscape is left to its own devices.

When diversity means plants of any global origin, as long as they grow well together and fit their respective niches, that can get a little troubling. If wildlife can't recognize or use the plant—if larvae can't eat the foliage or the pollen's nutritional content is not up to snuff compared to concurrently blooming native species—then the overall diversity of the functional landscape

As the climate warms, even drought-tolerant plants in the desert Southwest will be challenged. However, emulating natural conditions in the home garden may help plants and wildlife adapt—or at least hang on a bit longer. © Saxon Holt / PhotoBotanic. Used with permission.

Plants have fascinating adaptations. Take early-blooming pasque flower (*Anemone patens*): the fuzzy form acts like the hairs on our arms to insulate the plant, while colorful sepals close at night to protect pollen from frost and snow.

A seemingly simple sedge lawn in Santa Barbara, California, matches the home's aesthetic as it belies a resilient habitat. Sometimes "simple" may be what most benefits the site.

begins to suffer. Additionally, most invasive plant species have come from the exotic plant trade or from our gardens. How can we accurately predict when a plant will escape cultivation, become invasive, and reduce diversity beyond the garden fence?

Diversity for its own sake may not even be a helpful goal. In *Principles of Ecological Design*, Travis Beck shares a study that suggests having just six to sixteen plant species supports ecosystem function. He notes: "Apparent biodiversity of urban areas is not ecologically meaningful, as most landscape plantings are small, disconnected, limited to a few families of plants, and not structured to produce ecofunction. It must become operative to be ecologically meaningful, and for that to happen it needs to tie together built and remnant environments, it needs to be allowed to evolve and adapt, and it needs to provide services we need."

In other words, diversity—or biodiversity in the case of plant material—means a diversity of functional traits or niches that plants fill. Such biodiversity includes

Having a few species blooming at one time, and in larger numbers, not only provides for more efficient pollination but also shows more design intention. © Kevin O'Brien. Used with permission.

height, leaf size, woody, herbaceous, perennial, annual, evergreen, cool season, warm season, bloom time, and how the plant supports specific wildlife species.

Generally, Beck says, the more plants you have from the same ecoregion, the more ecosystem function you have. And further, the more plants you have from the same family within that landscape—like Asteraceae—the more ecosystem function there is. This is functional biodiversity, and it is our goal in creating regionally appropriate, nature-based gardens that reflect local plant communities. We can even narrow our plant selection further by considering bees and floral fidelity. When more of one species is blooming, we have more bees (even generalists) working that one species, which increases flower fertilization and helps bees use the garden more efficiently with less stress.

Without paying too much attention to aesthetic or site considerations just yet, what might a plant list look like for a garden such as the one above? It must include plants from various functional groups in the same ecoregion. For example:

Canada wild rye (*Elymus canadensis*)—cool-season grass
Little bluestem (*Schizachyrium scoparium*)—warm-season shortgrass
Indiangrass (*Sorghastrum nutans*)—warm-season tallgrass
Lead plant (*Amorpha canescens*)—woody nitrogen-fixing legume
Round headed bushclover (*Lespedeza capitata*)—nitrogen-fixing legume
Lanceleaf coreopsis (*Coreopsis lanceolata*)—summer bloom, aster family
Rough blazingstar (*Liatris aspera*)—late-summer bloom, aster family
Prairie rose (*Rosa arkansana*)—woody forb

The next step is to increase the range in each group, with varying habits and life cycles. So we might add to the above list:

Junegrass (*Koeleria macrantha*)—cool-season grass
Plains oval sedge (*Carex brevior*)—sedge
False blue indigo (*Baptisia australis*)—nitrogen-fixing legume with spring bloom
Early sunflower (*Heliopsis helianthoides*)—short-lived perennial, aster family
Black-eyed Susan (*Rudbeckia hirta*)—biennial, aster family
Common ironweed (*Vernonia fasciculata*)—late-summer perennial, aster family
Showy goldenrod (*Solidago speciosa*)—fall perennial, aster family

Some of these plants may be too tall or spread too easily for the intended space, so you'll need to make substitutions—all considerations we'll cover further as we explore the aesthetic and site demands of landscapes later in this chapter and the next.

Habit, Lifespan, Reproduction, Wildlife Support

Now that you know your ecoregion and have started to explore functional diversity, it's time to find the plants so you can begin researching which might work best in your given site conditions. We can start by picking up regional and state guidebooks, exploring resources on university extension websites, doing a simple zip code search via several nonprofit organizations, and then looking to USDA and Biota of North America Program (BONAP) range maps.

Let's say, just by throwing a dart at a map, you live in eastern Nebraska and have no idea what is native or what would work well in a garden setting. Here's one order of beginning research:

1. Type in your zip code to get plant lists from the Xerces Society, the Audubon Society, and Pollinator Partnership websites; the latter also has thirty-four regional guides that explore your area in greater detail. Then

Rattlesnake master (*Eryngium yuccifolium*) can behave differently depending on region and site conditions, such as plant density and soil moisture. Some report that it self-sows freely, others that it seldom does. Regardless, it's a consistent pollinator supporter.

look at the closest university extension website to see what online or print publications it has listing native plants for gardens. A wonderful public university in Nebraska has a wealth of information, especially via the Nebraska Statewide Arboretum (and much of its material would apply well beyond its level 3 ecoregion, by the way).

2. Pick up a state or regional native plant guidebook—a plethora of them exist, but a really good one is *Field Guide to Wildflowers of Nebraska and the Great Plains*. Since you have a basic plant list from the websites in step 1, these guidebooks will help you learn more details about those plants and whether they'd actually work on your specific site.

3. Having narrowed down the plant list, it's time to make sure these plants are native to your county via the USDA's plants database, which shows county-by-county distribution for each plant species. Another resource is BONAP, which goes into even more regional detail on historical flora, geography, climate, and other factors to help you learn more about the climate and region you're planting into.

4. To get as much information as you can to form a baseline of knowledge about how each plant performs in the landscape, type the scientific plant name into an internet search; never use common names, as they can apply to more than one species. The more local and regional the information source, the better, but you can still get a general baseline from reputable sources such as the Missouri Botanical Garden (MOBOT) and Lady Bird Johnson Wildflower Center. For the Midwest, little else beats Illinois Wildflowers, which also has a historical database on which insect species use which plant species.

Typing in the scientific name will get you myriad search results, some better than others, and over time, you'll intuitively learn which sources you can trust, including regional plant growers and native plant nurseries. Just remember that no one source is the be-all and end-all of information, and that as you create a baseline of plant performance across sources, results may vary in your beds based on a smattering of wild variables. But to plant nerds, uncertainty leads to deeper excitement, as nature teaches us more and more about how to adapt and thrive. When a beloved plant dies, you can try it again or find a new crush—either way, you're on the road to success.

Don't be afraid of the great black wasp (*Sphex pensylvanicus*)—they are solitary and docile, and they much prefer katydids over humans.

DANDELIONS ARE NOT THE FIRST FLOWER

It's good to leave dandelions (*Taraxacum officinale*) in spring and not spray them away—they will be used by a few generalist adult pollinators, for example—but they are far from the best source of nutrition. For example, the pollen of our native pussy willow has a protein count of 40 percent, compared to the dandelion's 14 percent. As native bees emerge in spring and mate, females are looking for pollen to feed their larvae—often from plants they evolved with. What are some native plants that bloom before and alongside dandelions?

Trees and Shrubs

- Pussy willow (*Salix discolor*)
- Red maple (*Acer rubrum*)
- Red elderberry (*Sambucus racemosa*)
- Currants or gooseberries (*Ribes* spp.)
- Wild plum (*Prunus americana*)
- Chokecherry (*Prunus virginiana*)
- Viburnum (*Viburnum* spp.)
- Dogwood (*Cornus* spp.)
- Serviceberry (*Amelanchier* spp.)

Prairie or Savanna Perennials and Biennials

- Prairie smoke (*Geum triflorum*)
- Pussytoes (*Antennaria neglecta*)
- Golden Alexanders (*Zizia* spp.)
- Wild lupine (*Lupinus perennis*)
- Pasque flower (*Anemone patens*)
- Marsh marigold (*Caltha palustris*)
- Early buttercup (*Ranunculus fascicularis*)
- Cleft phlox (*Phlox bifida*)
- Ground plum (*Astragalus crassicarpus*)
- Azure bluet (*Houstonia caerulea*)
- Longleaf bluet (*Houstonia longifolia*)
- Violet wood sorrel (*Oxalis violacea*)
- Prairie dandelion (*Nothocalais cuspidata*)
- Prairie blue-eyed grass (*Sisyrinchium campestre*)

Woodland Perennials and Ephemerals

- Bloodroot (*Sanguinaria canadensis*)
- Dutchman's breeches (*Dicentra cucullaria*)
- Native violets (*Viola* spp.)
- Jacob's ladder (*Polemonium reptans*)
- Large-flowered bellwort (*Uvularia grandiflora*)
- Wild geranium (*Geranium maculatum*)
- Bishop's cap (*Mitella diphylla*)
- Virginia bluebells (*Mertensia virginica*)
- Virginia waterleaf (*Hydrophyllum virginianum*)
- White trout lily (*Erytronium albidum*)
- Yellow trout lily (*Eryhronium americanum*)
- Spring beauty (*Claytonia virginica*)
- Sharp-lobed hepatica (*Hepatica acutiloba*)
- Robin's plantain (*Erigeron pulchellus*)
- Twinleaf (*Jeffersonia diphylla*)
- Early meadow rue (*Thalictrum dioicum*)
- Solomon's plume (*Maianthemum racemosum*)

Blue mistflower's (*Conoclinium coelestinum*) aggressive nature can be a benefit as it fills in gaps within the planting. Clay soil and healthy competition, especially from grasses, can help even the playing field.

So that's how you begin finding the right native plants for your garden. If this feels like overkill, please realize that it's really just the surface; the more you learn about a plant before digging it in, the more you can accept what's happening as your garden evolves as part of natural processes. For example, after planting a blue mistflower (*Conoclinum coelestinum*), if you wish it didn't run so much and are frustrated it isn't staying in a one-square-foot area, you could instead plan for this behavior and use it to your advantage to cover a weedy space a little faster or provide a nice drift of purple color late in August between two major bloom periods. Or, simply having done fifteen minutes of research on this plant, you know generally what to expect and can be assured you are gardening "right" and aren't a plant assassin.

Observing a site before planting is critical, too, and the more you can live with that site over a few seasons, the better. If you note how water flows, where light falls—how light falls (dappled, straight, reflected), when (time of day, time of year) and for how long—current weed pressure or other vegetative growth, slope, soil type, and where winter snow gathers, all these can be helpful clues as to what plant characteristics to look for. You can also find a wilder area in your locale that exhibits most of these site characteristics and catalog what is growing there, going home to research the plants and their communities in more detail. Many apps can identify a plant—Google Lens works for me at least half the time—and even if it's not precise, you can generally figure out a plant name by knowing what it looks like. There's something to be said for multiple internet search strings, no matter how wordy; for example, "yellow flowering weed in central Ohio that blooms in June, has glossy leaves, and is short" once brought up the exact plant I was looking for right off the bat.

Plant Communities and Layers

Perhaps one of the most important terms to learn is "plant community," simply because it reflects an entirely new relationship with garden design. And since I've already mentioned plant communities repeatedly, it's high time to explore this term in more detail. What is a plant community? It's a conglomeration of plants where both exclusion and mutualism, and competition and sharing, have created a relatively stable ecosystem. It's stable in the sense that no one species dominates at the expense of others, and if a few species vanish due to drought or disease, others can move in and fill the niche without a significant loss of ecosystem function. So "stable" means "resilient," which home gardeners might also call "low maintenance." Now, such ecosystem function and resilience can include stabilizing soil, reducing runoff, providing wildlife

In a tallgrass prairie, these three plants, all aggressive in nature, work together to create resilience because of their similar behavior: big bluestem, Canadian goldenrod, and tall boneset (*Eupatorium altissimum*).

This scene of pale purple coneflower (*Echinacea pallida*), at Schulenberg prairie in suburban Chicago, provides gardeners a design cue on how to replicate a scattering of blooms in a smaller landscape. © Paul Westervelt. Used with permission.

When scaled down to size, as in this modest suburban bed, lessons taken from larger prairies can be translated for an effective ecology and aesthetic. Instead of coneflowers dotting the entire landscape (in this case, *Echinacea purpurea*), a few clumps repeat themselves.

habitat, and a host of other benefits. In case you haven't been paying attention, this is exactly how a prairie works and why it's important to study how prairies grow and evolve.

A community of plants is working together—or the plants are working against one another—to maintain an ecosystem. These plants may play nice, or their aggression may be held in check by other aggressive species; either way, there's a sense of dynamic stability in which the composition may change from year to year, but the site retains its overall ecosystem function. In essence, it looks the same from year to year on a drive-by, but spend a few moments cataloging plant species, and you'll notice how the composition has shifted.

This reality is key to creating a nature-inspired garden. The goal is not just an aesthetic collection of decorator items; it's a collection of beautiful and functional plant species whose very natures are harnessed to create a stylized, interpreted wildness that supports local biodiversity and that works in a more structured home garden.

Think back to the previous chapter when we were discussing prairie, plant density, and competition. Here's John Weaver again:

So many species—often a total of 200 or more per square mile—can exist together only by sharing the soil at different levels, by obtaining light at different heights, and by making maximum demands for water, nutrients, and light at different seasons of the year. Legumes add nitrogen to the soil; tall plants protect the lower ones from the heating and drying effects of full insolation; and the mat formers and other prostrate species further reduce water loss by covering the soil's surface, living in an atmosphere that is much better supplied with moisture than are the windswept plants above them. Light is absorbed at many levels; the more-or-less-vertical leaves of the dominant grasses permit light to filter between them as the sun swings across the heaven. Compared with crops of wheat or maize, fluctuations in temperature of both soil and air are much less in prairie, humidity is consistently higher, and evaporation is decreased. The prairie's demands for water and light increase more gradually and extend over a longer period of time.

The point of all this is to find guides to gardening with nature and not against it by using endemic plant communities. If we understand the region we grow in, and the native plants therein, we will have a much better idea of how to garden and how to manage that garden, even in an evolving climate. When we can do all that, our expectations change, and then our gardens begin to do more work for all of us together. If we can start to see something like stress as an asset in our gardens instead of an impediment to overcome, gardening suddenly means something new. As Thomas Rainer and Claudia West say in their book *Planting in a Post-Wild World*: "The irony is that what we perceive as happy, well-adjusted plants is more often the result of a scarcity of resources rather than an abundance of it."

A wild plant community in autumn shows off some of the more charismatic species that have self-organized: little bluestem, grey-head coneflower, and heath aster. Other species include prairie wild rose (*Rosa arkansana*), stiff goldenrod (*Oligoneuron rigidum*), and golden Alexanders (*Zizia aurea*). Noting the habits and arrangement of these plants can clue us in to how they create dynamic stability.

A mass of a certain plant produces more seedlings than can possibly survive, which means only the fittest continue on. This natural selection is what we're after.

So let's ask the question again: what is a plant community? In one square yard of healthy prairie, dozens of plant species coexist. We can't possibly hope to replicate this in a home garden, and even if we did, it might be too "weedy." But we can observe the prairie layers at work and what plants are growing together, and through researching each plant's natural tendencies, we can begin to create a rudimentary and pared-down palette that can work in a more stylized garden bed.

A prairie restoration typifies what self-organized plants can teach us as we bring a little wildness home. Butterflyweed (*Asclepias tuberosa*) prefers to grow singly, golden Alexanders (*Zizia aurea*) are in larger drifts, while *Ratibida pinnata* and *Dalea purpurea* are in smaller groups. Little bluestem and sideoats grama form the green mulch or matrix. Bringing these plant groupings down to scale while increasing floral density is what natural garden design is about.

The first aspect we notice about a prairie or meadow is how green it is, and how most plants share the same green hue. It's pleasing, calming, and even ordered. There's a benefit to this green uniformity when we think about color theory, as a consistent green is seen as readable and calming—hence we have so many lawns, and hence we may want to limit ourselves to one or two green hues in our natural landscapes, so it's easier for others to see intent and order. It might be easy to assume that green represents only a few dominant plant species, or that to have the kind of pleasing uniformity we crave in designed landscapes, we should rely on only a few species. But in an artistic, resilient habitat garden, that's not the case. This type of garden contains layers of plants, layers of seasonality, and layers of succession we need to understand in creating a nature-based landscape full of sustainable plant communities.

A more intentional display garden flanks a restored tallgrass prairie. It's easy to see what lessons have been taken from the prairie beyond and incorporated into the foreground, such as a uniform structure and color underlying punctuations of ornamental forbs.

Layers of Plants

First, I want you to think about gardens you've visited and admired. Most likely you're reminiscing about a space that wowed you, that you described to someone else as "beautiful" and "lush." Now, did that garden have just a single layer of plants, only one plant in an entire bed? Likely not—but if it did, that would be a high-maintenance landscape requiring constant weeding and fidgeting. Just like gardens, prairies have layers: groundcovers, mid-level structural plants, and taller architectural plants. These categories can be broken down even further, of course, but for our purposes, this is enough. A plant at each layer is living in its niche, doing what it evolved to do. A natural garden has several plants at each layer, as well as plants doing their thing at different times of year.

Some plants hug the ground or grow very low; these might include sedges (*Carex* spp.), pasque flower (*Anemone patens*), geranium, short grasses, and

The Lurie Garden in Chicago exemplifies a highly designed assemblage of plant layers, as well as layers of seasonality from spring through winter. The landscape contains both native and exotic plants and is above a parking structure, acting as a green roof.

A spring landscape perhaps more easily shows the developing layers. In a month's time, the tall, architectural layers will have surpassed shorter plant species, while fall-blooming plants will still be ramping up their growth. © Andrew Marrs Garden Design. Used with permission.

This shade meadow at Crystal Bridges Museum of American Art illustrates that woodland gardens have layers as stunning and ecologically purposeful as their sunnier counterparts. Golden groundsel (*Packera aurea*) is thriving.

poppy mallow (*Callirhoe* spp.). Then the next layer is where we see taller forbs with seasonal attributes, like milkweed (*Asclepias* spp.), aster (*Symphyotrichum* spp.), coneflower (*Echinacea* spp.), mountain mint (*Pycnanthemum* spp.), tickseed (*Coreopsis* spp.), and prairie clover (*Dalea* spp.)—species that generally have smaller populations than the ground layers. These mid-level plants all act as buttresses for taller species and as the primary seasonal color show as the growing season progresses. Finally, we have taller plants whose form might be more sculptural and whose populations are generally the smallest or more sporadic: ironweed (*Vernonia* spp.), compass plant (*Silphium laciniatum*), late boneset (*Eupatorium serotinum*), and white false indigo (*Baptisia alba*).

Purple prairie clover (*Dalea purpurea*) has a woody taproot that can reach 5–7 feet down; it is considered a mid- to late successional species of healthy landscapes. The Pawnee used its dried stems as a broom, and the Oglala Sioux brewed a tea from its leaves.

These plants fill niches not only above ground but also beneath the soil line. An Allium (bulb) or Liatris (corm) do not compete for the same resources as a little bluestem, because their root masses are in different soil profiles or layers underground. A taprooted coneflower is doing something very different from fibrous-rooted sedge, and if grown together, they won't compete so much as fill niches that amend soil while outcompeting weeds for resources. As much as we see and plan for layers above ground, we should also consider the layers underground if we're planning on resilience, ecosystem function, and sustainability. The more root diversity we have, the more life we create in all layers.

Layers of Seasonality

If everything in nature bloomed at once, a lot of fauna would be in trouble. And we'd have more boring landscapes. Seasonality applies not only to when a species flowers but also to when species reach their maturity—so think height,

Prairie blazingstar (*Liatris pycnostachya*).

Prairie alumroot (*Heuchera richardsonii*).

seed heads, and even fall color. When we plan for seasonality in a garden, we plan for not only aesthetic interest but also ecosystem function.

For example, some plants complete their annual life cycle by late spring or early summer—just consider woodland or woodland edge ephemerals, as well as some prairie species such as pasque flower. Many spring perennials go to seed as warm-season bunchgrasses leap from the ground, including wild columbine. Ensuring that something is always in bloom provides not only beauty for us but also resources for pollinators and those species that depend on pollinators as a food source, including spiders, wasps, and birds. Keep in

Compass plant (*Silphium laciniatum*).

Switchgrass (*Panicum virgatum*).

mind, many specialist bees also depend on their preferred plants being present and in bloom, timing their life cycles around flowering periods.

And then there's fall color, because most plants—even including herbaceous perennials—show remarkable fall coloration as they go dormant. Some of my favorite autumn herbaceous perennials for leaf color include rattlesnake master, wild geranium (*Geranium maculatum*), coreopsis, swamp milkweed (*Asclepias incarnata*), blazingstar (*Liatris* spp.), wild bergamot (*Monarda fistulosa*), and indiangrass (*Sorghastrum nutans*). Going further, a plethora of plants have rather showy seed heads or winter shape, or they provide valuable wildlife forage—so seasonality is something that can get quite complex but also infinitely exciting.

Meadow blazingstar (*Liatris ligulistylis*).

Dwarf blue indigo (*Baptisia australis minor*).

Purple prairie clover.

Virginia mountain mint.

Morning in a winter garden can often lead to rime, which is the result of freezing fog.

Dwarf blue indigo foliage gives new meaning to winter interest.

PERENNIAL FORBS WITH ORNAMENTAL WINTER SEED HEADS OR BRACTS

Eryngium yuccifolium
Pycnanthemum spp.
Lespedeza capitata
Oligoneuron rigidum
Symphyotrichum spp.
Vernonia spp.
Liatris spp.
Amsonia spp.
Baptisia spp.
Agastache foeniculum
Veronicastrum virginicum
Echinacea spp.
Rudbeckia spp.
Eutrochium spp.
Monarda spp.
Senna hebecarpa

Layers of Succession

Plants never remain as they are, either as lone specimens or in colonies. All sorts of pressures exert change, from climate to weather to herbivores to fire. Year over year, the plant composition changes, but so do the natures of specific plant species. As they grow and flower, many aster and monarda species get open and leggy. What shorter species might underplant them to keep the ground covered and provide maximum ecosystem function and habitat?

Other species tend to be early colonizers in a new seeding or planted bed that fade out over time, including forbs such as gray-headed coneflower, black-eyed Susan, and Mexican hat. These early successional or pioneer plants can help stabilize the ecosystem while additional community members get es-

Wild bergamot and grayhead coneflower put on a stunning flower show when paired together in young gardens.

A sequence of images from the spring cut down to early winter highlights a garden's seasonal evolution.

tablished. Other plants take years before they flower, working first on roots: consider false indigo and compass plant. If we want to include these plants, we need to be patient and ensure they aren't outcompeted early on.

Planning for succession means understanding how long plants live, how they reproduce, and how they fare in a tightly woven community. For example, black-eyed Susans, while tending to act like a biennial, diminish in number as plant layers mature around them—there's just less light hitting the ground for seed germination while roots of neighboring plants also scramble for soil resources. But place black-eyed Susan in an open, mulched bed, and it will become a black-eyed Susan bed almost in perpetuity—which is beautiful for a while, but come late summer, the plant dies and there's little else to slow erosion, stop weeds, or provide pollen for insects.

So succession means considering which plants will come online first, which will proliferate and fade, and which will take a few years to develop. If you'd like to go a step further, succession also includes how plants propagate or how aggressive they might be. You may find plants that spread more locally by root are better suited to your landscape than those that spread widely by seed. More than likely, you'll have to learn many of these principles by observation or by trial and error, because the plant community, environment, site conditions, and climate can make a plant act differently from what research suggests. Even a neighbor's hyssop down the street may perform differently from the one in your garden. Maybe this is why so many commercial landscapes are rather simple and dominated by the same plant species and swaths of wood mulch: they are more easily controlled and predictable.

One caveat to this entire conversation about layers is that any disturbance will reset the table, and that is often a very good and necessary thing. Sometimes disturbance is intentional, to increase diversity and flowers (mowing and fire) or to knock back an aggressive species, while sometimes it's unintentional (climate, weather, or disease). Knowing how plants grow—and how they compete—can help us decide how and when to create disturbance to increase the ecological function of layers and maintain resilience alongside diversity. This is what land managers do over hundreds and thousands of acres of prairie, and to some extent, it's something we need to consider when managing a few hundred or thousand square feet. In the next two chapters, we'll explore in more detail how to do this with specific plant compositions as we plan, install, and manage a landscaped bed.

A foundation bed garden in its second year that includes Virginia mountain mint (*Pycnanthemum virginianum*), black-eyed Susan (*Rudbeckia hirta*), purple coneflower (*Echiancea purpurea*), meadow blazingstar (*Liatris ligulistylis*), plains oval sedge (*Carex brevior*), and little bluestem (*Schizachyrium scoparium*). © Valerie Rivera. Used with permission.

3

PLANNING, INSTALLING, AND MANAGING THE GARDEN

"There is sometimes a misperception that designing with native plant communities and natural processes is not sufficiently artful. In reality, it can be considered to be a new art form appropriate to the 21st century: 'ecological art,' which is simultaneously aesthetically rich, ecologically sound, evocative of place, and dynamic."
—DARREL MORRISON

Believe it or not, once you have a plant list, some of the hardest work is done. You've accomplished the necessary research to know what plants would be best suited to your site, and you've come to get a baseline on how each plant performs—including height, width, method of reproduction, and rooting behavior. Nothing can replace the knowledge you have attained, and you are prepared to learn exponentially as the years unfold. You've got a huge leg up! Now the really fun part can begin: creating a layout, install, and management strategy.

The basic criteria for plant selection have always been: texture, leaf color, bloom color, and size. In a more natural garden, those criteria are joined by aspects of ecological function, including ability to slow erosion, increase water absorption, mitigate weeds, and provide for specific wildlife, among many others. As we find the plants best suited for our site conditions and goals,

In general, the term "texture" means the diversity of contrasting plant foliage. Here, early summer shows off the rich interplay of *Eryngium yuccifolium* (smooth blue-green lances), *Dalea purpurea* (erect, lacy stems), and the underlying matrix of *Bouteloua curtipendula* (feathery leaves).

we are inherently creating a landscape plan; the next step is figuring out actual composition and placement.

There are two primary ways to create a landscape plan: the first is drawing it freehand or with a computer program, or simply laying out plants on site. Any drawing program or app will do, but I've come to prefer SketchUp because it's easy to move around plant icons. For larger, complex projects I find using a drawing helpful, so I can match plant habits, create functional plant communities, and calculate how many of each species I'll need. However, for smaller beds, I am experienced enough to know how a core group of plants I frequently use will grow, and I prefer to feel the space in situ as I lay out and move plants in artistic yet purposeful ecological communities. Such a process can take thirty minutes for a small bed, or hours or even days for larger ones. With any approach, grouping your plants on paper or spreadsheet into several subheadings can help you get a feel for how you want to use them and which will be placed next to which; this is where we expand on the basic texture, color, and size list:

Spring bloom
Early-midsummer bloom
Late-summer bloom
Fall bloom
Early succession
Late succession

Architectural plants
Groundcover plants
Seasonal plants
Fall and winter seed heads
Root behavior
Competitiveness or sociability

The categories on bloom time should be self-explanatory, but some of the others may need clarification. Architectural plants tend to be taller and / or provide some unique shape. I often think of such plants as trees and shrubs or

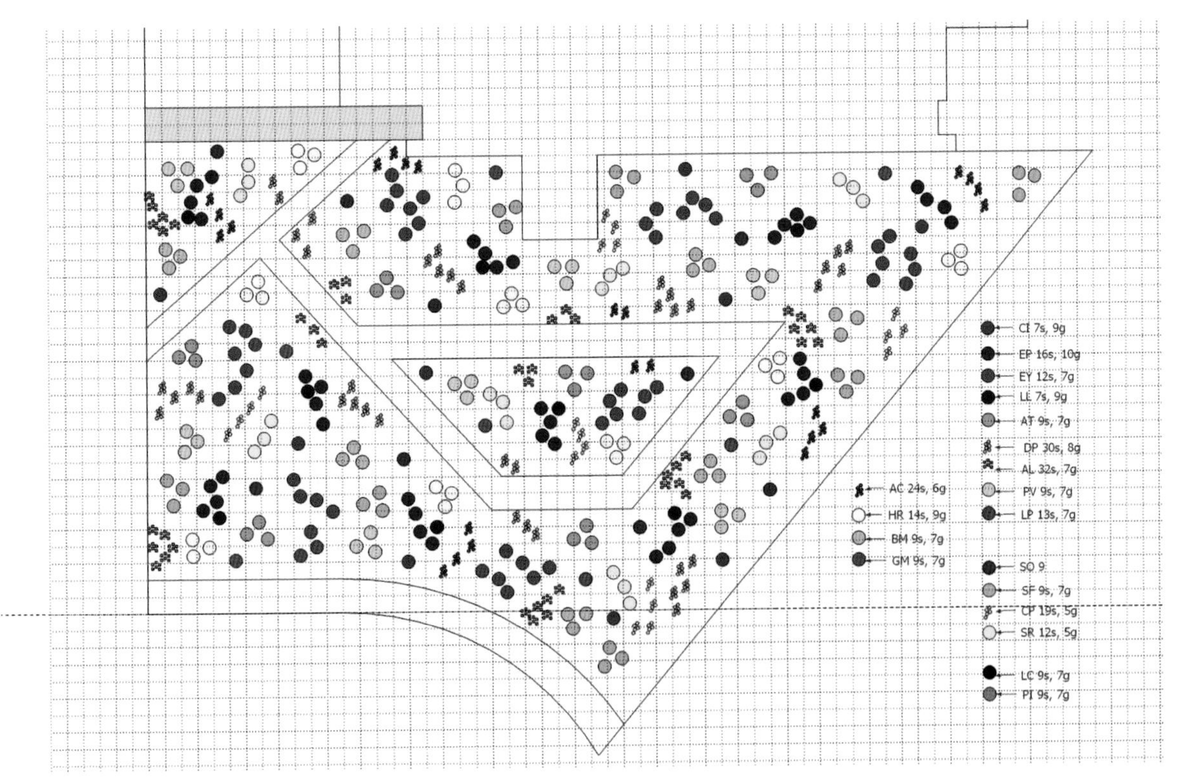

Using a grid that marks square footage helps in making plant placement and building the communities. This was created using SketchUp.

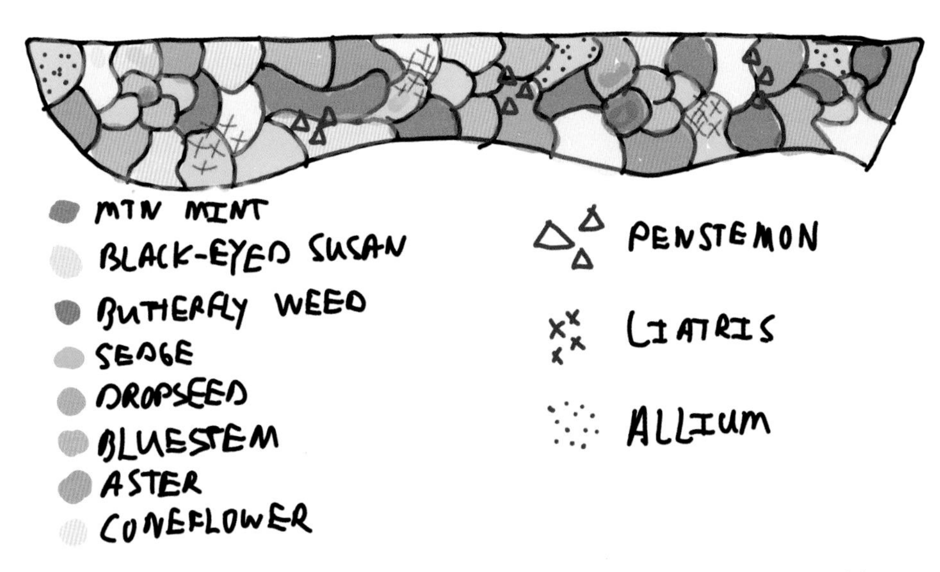

Freehand doodling works, too; this garden was laid out using an app on a tablet.

towering herbaceous perennials; these plants are not likely to dominate the design, as we'll see in our sample plans in chapter 4.

Seasonal plants are those that carry the foliage, flower, or seed head load in respective seasons, and they likely will be more of a middle layer comprising the second-most number of plants. Here, some plants that fit the category could be purple prairie clover (*Dalea purpurea*), pale purple coneflower (*Echinacea pallida*), mountain mint (*Pycnanthemum virginanum*), smooth aster (*Symphyotrichum laeve*), prairie coreopsis (*Coreopsis palmata*), wild columbine (*Aquilegia canadensis*), golden Alexanders (*Zizia aurea*), and zigzag goldenrod (*Solidago flexicaulis*). Another category of seasonal plants would be those with showy winter seed heads or umbels, of which round-headed bush clover (*Lespedeza capitata*) and stiff goldenrod (*Oligoneuron rigidum*) are favorites.

Once on site, it can be helpful to spray-paint where plants will go, especially when you're using helpers.

Groundcover plants can be a range of species, from wild geranium and winecups (*Callirhoe involucrata*) to bunchgrasses, rushes and sedge. The plants may be as numerous as or more numerous than the seasonal plant category, and we'll explore such plants and their ecological uses more when we discuss matrix garden design a little further ahead.

For competitiveness and sociability, one of the best methods is a 1–4 ranking. Since you've done some thorough plant research, you've got a pretty good idea of how plants will spread, how fast, and in what site conditions. Of course, nothing can beat observation over the years, but until you have that experience, you won't be able to fine-tune. A level 1 sociability ranking is a plant that is a behaved clumper; level 2 is one that lightly spreads to form a small grouping; level 3 is a plant that's more aggressive, either creating a larger mass or appearing easily in new spots throughout the bed; finally, level 4 is a very aggressive species that, over time, may attempt to produce a monoculture if not placed

Round-headed bush clover (*Lespedeza capitata*) mixed in with a stand of indiangrass (*Sorghastrum nutans*); both could be considered architectural plants.

With low basal foliage and spring flowers that turn into glittery seed heads, prairie smoke (*Geum triflorum*) is an ideal groundcover species.

Butterflyweed (*Asclepias tuberosa*) provides bright color in summer, ornamental seed pods in fall, and a modest stature that makes it a good choice for front-yard prairie conversions; it's a seasonal filler.

In this diverse mixture, both native and exotic species have been matched to one another to create seasonal layers based on habit. By fall, each plant's form has been fully realized and the garden takes on new aesthetic and ecological roles. © Andrew Marrs Garden Design. Used with permission.

with other similarly competitive species. Further adding nuance to this scale: some species, especially those with root runners, may be less aggressive in dense clay than loose loam. It should go without saying that placing a 1 next to a 4 is not in your best interest. In a small bed, having all level 1 or 2 species is a solid plan, while in a larger bed or one with significant weed pressure, 3 and 4 are potentially desirable. If you have an aggressive, architectural species in a small bed in your front yard, you can safely bet the farm that in a few years, you will be reported to weed control. I'm looking at you, common milkweed (*Asclepias syriaca*) and maximillian sunflower (*Helianthus maximiliani*).

Common wood sedge (*Carex blanda*) is a moderately aggressive species ideally suited to shade gardens or under the shadow of taller plants in a sunnier meadow. Many sedge species make excellent groundcovers and fillers.

Ivory sedge (*Carex eburnea*) spreads at a moderately slow rate in clay soil, and it stays very close to the ground in dry shade conditions. It's like a troll-doll head convention.

PLANT SOCIABILITY

The following example lists perennial competitiveness and aggressiveness on a 1–4 scale when placed in a tightly planted, layered bed of medium-moisture, clay soil in 75 percent or more sun:

Level 1

Prairie alumroot (*Heuchera richardsonii*)
Butterfly milkweed (*Asclepias tuberosa*)
Rough blazingstar (*Liatris aspera*)
Dwarf false indigo (*Baptisia minor*)

Level 2

Purple coneflower (*Echinacea purpurea*)
Sideoats grama (*Bouteloua curtipendula*)
Rattlesnake master (*Eryngium yuccifolium*)
Poppy mallow (*Callirhoe involucrata*)

Level 3

Little bluestem (*Schizachyrium scoparium*)
Smooth aster (*Symphyotrichum laeve*)
Blue mistflower (*Conoclinium coelestinum*)
Virginia mountain mint (*Pycnanthemum virginianum*)

Level 4

Fox sedge (*Carex vulpinoidea*)
Canada goldenrod (*Solidago canadensis*)
Anise hyssop (*Agastache foeniculum*)
Indiangrass (*Sorghastrum nutans*)

Not only will creating these lists allow you to further hone your understanding of specific plants, but it will also help you create a more low-management space that functions as a stable, resilient, wildlife-supportive, designed ecosystem that appeals aesthetically to others. That last point is especially important if you live in a neighborhood with a homeowners association (HOA).

Intentionality in natural gardens can take on many levels: for example, using concurrently blooming species that share similar flower color, or flowers that pick up on foliage hues from nearby grasses or other perennials. © Austin Eischeid Garden Design and Jensen Ecology. Used with permission.

On HOAs

While some HOAs are fairly loose and flexible, others require stringent planning and presenting of your proposed project. The more you know your plants, the more you can convince others that you know what you're doing and that the outcomes will be in line with everyone's expectations. By creating lists of plants, you'll get a better feel for which plant to use, which to cut out, how to arrange the plants, and how to plan for bloom and plant succession that mitigates some of the inevitable complaints of weediness even in small foundation beds.

Here's what I'd bring to a conversation with a strict HOA board:

1. A plant list with scientific and common names, including images of each plant.
2. A table of bloom times, color, and anticipated mature size.
3. A table of plant sociability (for example, you won't be using aggressive plants).
4. Images of inspirational gardens by landscape design firms you hope to emulate.
5. The specific wildlife benefits of each plant (milkweed for monarch egg laying: "As you all probably know, monarch populations are down X percent in our region," or "The loss of pollinators, like bees, has been in the news, and these specific plants have been shown in this scientific study to provide the best pollen for insects."
6. The specific neighborhood benefits: trees that shade hard surfaces like streets and roofs, which decreases those surface temperatures by X percent; increased value of homes and desirability of neighborhoods as perceived by buyers; thick, layered garden beds reduce storm runoff that could overwhelm drains and carry pollutants into nearby ponds and streams; kids who live in a more biodiverse neighborhood have fewer allergies and improved mental health. Less lawn = less fertilizer and less noise pollution (you might include stats on the harm fertilizer does to local waterways, the toxic side effects of mower exhaust, how loud a mower is and how long it takes that level of noise to cause hearing damage).
7. A planting plan—even if you don't stick with it 100 percent—showing placement of each and every plant, no matter how tedious that will be.
8. A detailed management plan by season (when you will cut back, when you will replant, what you will be looking for as you manage, and how often you will weed).
9. Obvious areas for a table, bench, walking path, or pergola in your design.
10. Signatures of neighbors who approve of your plan.
11. Awareness of local weed ordinances and prepared rebuttals for the most common points of concern: fire and pests (such as snakes and rodents).
12. Approval of the plan by the city or county weed superintendent.

All that being said, if you have a well-organized HOA, you probably need to be twice as organized to move your "wilder" garden plan forward. It may be worth your time and money to hire a consultant or designer to draw up a basic plan and at least provide a written methodology, if not to attend a board presentation with you as your wingman. I encourage you not to give up too

Suburban tract housing often leaves a lot to be desired when it comes to sustainability, resilience, and habitat. But each lot can begin to rebuild connectivity and ecosystem function, often extending nearby woodlands or meadows. The place to make a difference is where you live, and then you can go from there.

A modest foundation bed can both be natural and show intention. Here, repetition as well as a matching bloom palette help the bed appear tidy. Note that the taller species are placed in the background (*Eutrochium*, *Baptisia*). © Andrew Marrs Garden Design. Used with permission.

quickly or early in the bureaucratic process, because few things in life that are worthwhile are easy; the more examples we have of a new landscape paradigm, the more folks can get used to the idea and slowly accept the inevitable change to seeing "weediness" as caring for the community.

HOW TO PASS WEED INSPECTION

My local superintendent said they have to respond to all complaints submitted via their online system, which means they automatically send out temporary summer help to take a photo and post a sign in your landscape. Those summer inspectors don't do a site analysis, such as plant identification, so ultimately it's up to you to educate and work with neighbors and weed control. Here are some tips on creating that change with your local enforcers:

1. Never become angry or irrational in any communication. Maintain a calm, professional, even appreciative tone for weed control's work in all written and verbal communication.
   Don't email the superintendent saying: "Yesterday I received a rude and threatening letter about my pollinator garden. I am disgusted that you don't see the value of what I'm doing, as our environment is in peril. I am growing milkweed for monarchs, and as you should know, monarchs are in trouble. Do you hate nature?" Following a statement such as this one with several additional paragraphs won't move any needles.
   A more effective example might go like this: "On May 20th, I received a notice that the property I own at X address is in violation of city weed ordinances. I appreciate the work you do in monitoring our landscapes for invasive weeds and overgrown sites that may cause hazards to the public, and I look forward to working with you to resolve the issues on my site. As such, I am including a plant list for my garden beds, and I would welcome a visit to my landscape to discuss how I can come into compliance while maintaining ecosystem function for a healthy community of both wildlife and people."
2. Tidy up before any visit by the superintendent or lead inspector (mow, trim, paint a fence) and bone up on your scientific plant names so you can name each species on demand.
3. Research local weed ordinances and prepare information that addresses common issues: invasive weed control (list invasive species that you do eradicate); pests such as rats and snakes (the former are attracted to human waste food, not plant seeds, and the latter are beneficial predators that eat the former).
4. Research legal precedents in your city and in others around the country. There are more and more each year.
5. During the site visit, be willing to make compromises. Sometimes a plant really is blocking sight lines or is too aggressive. And sometimes your landscape really is messy. Be open. Be calm. Be thankful.

6. Use your research to explain the benefits of your space: pollinator and bird support (bonus points for specific threatened species you've seen visit and what plants they use), benefits of leaving the garden up for winter, stormwater runoff mitigation (even in winter, as water still collects on leaves and stems rather than sliding off the frozen soil into storm drains).

And to reiterate: don't give up, and don't be a jerk. Our conversation here about HOAs and weed inspectors isn't meant to dissuade you from turning the tide and making a difference, but to embolden and empower as we design landscapes that are beautiful to both wildlife and people in dozens of ways.

On Weediness

The whole reason you might get into conflict with neighbors or inspectors is because of how we interpret weediness. What makes a garden weedy? While it can be as subjective as asking what makes a garden beautiful, in general, the following list covers most of the criteria:

- Plants that get too tall or flop
- Plants that spread too freely
- A design that does not employ massing and drifting
- Not tiering plants (taller ones in back or in the middle of a bed)
- A design that you can't see over or that blocks an important view
- Having too many plants in bloom at once (a limited number of species in bloom at any one time, say three or four, is a good general rule, particularly for smaller landscapes)
- Not ensuring something is always in bloom from spring to fall
- Not employing "cues to care" (a term coined by Joan Nassauer in her piece *Messy Ecosystems, Orderly Frames*), which are entry points for people to see the space as welcoming and purposeful. Such cues to care could be tables, paths, benches, arbors, sculptures, and signs that explain the garden's purpose.

Our goal should be to not have a weedy garden, and yet our goal is also to inspire a change in what defines weediness. Very few people I know would call a forest or prairie weedy, so it's up to us to interpret and even pare down the core elements of these wilder landscapes that we don't find weedy as we emulate them in urban areas. I think in general, the simpler your landscape—given its smaller size when compared to a prairie—the better off you may be. Consider what helps you see a wild landscape as cohesive and even approachable. Likely at the top of that list is repetition of the same plants as well as negative space

Employing traditional aspects of design—such as masses and tiers—can help show intention. Here, *Pycnanthemum muticum* fills gaps leading up to structural woody plants like sumac (*Rhus* spp.) and bottlebrush buckeye (*Aesculus parviflora*). © Richard A. McCoy / McCoy Horticultural. Used with permission.

Weedy or not? Our perceptions come filtered through cultural and social experiences; if we see more examples of the semi-wild and learn their benefits, we're much more likely to be accepting and encouraging.

Above left: Cues to care in a natural garden provide visual anchors and clue us in to purpose. Strategically placed arbors, fountains, stone paths, sculptures, and benches all make a difference.

Above right: One piece of art may be enough to show that this backyard meadow was planned and is welcoming to us.

Left: A single sheet of corten steel acts as a foil—something seemingly opposite but that elevates the readability of a wilder backyard landscape.

Lawn paths have several practical functions, such as access and serving as a firebreak.

Even a small bed can employ several design strategies to show intention: negative space (the sedge groundcover), bench, and plant tiers.

(open area, path, sitting area) that gives your eye a calm place to rest and re-set. Reducing species from twenty to fifteen or ten—at least initially—may be helpful, as would reducing the taller seasonal species while you increase the ground layer plants, so diversity and ecosystem function are still maintained. Mitigating weediness means knowing your plants, but when it comes to placing those plants in a bed, it also means understanding what design system or approach you will use.

Three Garden Design Approaches

Overall, there are generally three ways to design and lay out a nature-based, prairie-inspired landscape where we negotiate different levels of weediness: random mix, modular, and block planting. Each will always have its nuances.

If you toss out a bag of seed, you're going to get a random garden. This is not what you want in a front yard or highly visible space where neighbors may be close by. While it may be fun to watch as it evolves, and it is the most cost effective approach, it will get you into the most trouble with weed control. And never, ever buy a "pollinator mix" off a store shelf; these mixes tend to use lots of non-native species, early successional plants, and annuals, and not all species will be suited to your site conditions. This presents a host of management issues. Annuals—the cheapest option for a seed mix—will soon fade away, and without the right perennial competition, weeds will move in to fill the vacancy, and you'll have to start over. It's much better, if you are seeding, to design your own mix or at least use a reputable native plant nursery to help you design the mix. Many native plant growers even have their own mixes tailored for their region and to various site conditions, which is always a better bet than something purchased off the shelf (for more on custom seed mixes, see chapter 4).

Now, of course you can plant potted material in a randomized garden. You'll get results faster and have even more control over species and placement than you will when seeding. But this approach will still create issues with neighbors who may have traditional landscapes. One potential strategy is to use a few of the species in large masses, but that may leave yourself open to battles you may not want to fight.

A modular garden presents some middle ground, especially for larger spaces that are highly visible. Let's say you have 3,000' of space to design, but you don't have the time or experience to thoughtfully map out thousands of plants individually, and you prefer a more semi-wild look. In comes the module—a 100–200' garden square you design on paper, then replicate over and over until the larger space is filled. The benefit of this plan is that it makes planting simpler—good if you have helpers—and it creates a cohesive repetition throughout the space that shows a bit more order and purpose to anyone walking by. The plants are generally allowed to find their way from their starting points, and editing is as minimal or as hands-on as you wish. We'll look at modular garden design more in the next chapter as we explore plans for various site conditions.

The final approach to designing your garden is block planting, which is probably the most frequent way we garden. In block planting, you place homogeneous groups of plants right next to each other. The advantage is that it's highly and obviously stylized, whereas the downside is it's more open to weed invasion and less functional than a prairie-inspired, habitat-driven approach with layers. Block planting is quite popular in urban areas around business parks, downtown entertainment districts, and even botanical gardens, but it often does not have the long-term financial support needed for management (weed-

Planting in single-layer groups helps show design intention but can also require higher maintenance, including weeding and mulching. It's important to consider what design and management strategy will work best for you before making plant selections.

ing, specimen replacement) and / or it is maintained using pre-emergent herbicides, which means plants can't reproduce, fill in, and create a more stable and resilient bed. You'll also see block planting in public show gardens composed of annual plants that are changed out seasonally and cleaned out in autumn; these annual gardens do not support nearly as much wildlife and have reduced ecosystem services, such as carbon sequestration.

Probably your best approach is a modular design, even if you end up not repeating the module but instead expanding it or, more simply, learning how to lay out plants in a smaller area. While a modular design can include any style of planting—such as formal, block planting, and informal randomization—for our purposes, a full-on matrix may be best.

Matrix garden design uses one or several species that serve as a living green mulch, or ground layer, through which ornamental, usually flowering plants placed in masses emerge throughout the year. In a matrix, the occasional weed is less likely to get noticed or cause a problem due to plant density, whereas in a block planting, it will stand out like a lighthouse. You still employ plant community strategies in a matrix—layers of seasonality and succession—but you also increase habitat and ecosystem function, while minimizing management in future years. In some respects, matrix gardening allies closest with prairie and meadow structure.

Enter the Matrix

A matrix truly is the simplest way to approach nature-based, prairie-inspired garden design. And that's not to say it's lazy or easy, but it's approachable, scalable, and somewhat natural. I can't think of a better introduction to the kind of garden we're exploring in this book—it's certainly better than the traditional method of reading a plant tag and placing it in a bed where you think it might work, marooning it in wood mulch, and then hoping for the best.

The two primary ways to create a matrix are planting and seeding. You can plant plugs of a bunchgrass or sedge on 12" centers across the entire space for the green mulch, then fill in your ornamental masses and drifts of layered plant communities. A more affordable option is to place your ornamental layers—the seasonal bloomers and architectural plants—and then seed in a groundcover, such as a warm-season bunchgrass. The latter is more cost efficient but takes a little longer to establish. Keep in mind that the goal in planting the ornamental, seasonal, and architectural layers is to maintain the design, to meet people in the middle by showing purpose and intent. The matrix itself serves as the unifying structure, doing the work we discussed on color theory in the previous chapter.

Planting a matrix of plugs on 12" centers is pretty self-explanatory, with the caveat that warm-season grasses tend to do better plugged in spring or early fall rather than late fall. Matrix gardening takes advantage of natural plant behaviors to cover the ground quickly in lush layers, which increases ecosystem function. How you manage the matrix—by addition or subtraction or standing back—is gardening.

When laying out a matrix, it's easy to trip on the tightly spaced plants or wonder if it will work.

But, after a year or two, the rewards are many, as the ground is covered and the plant communities are ready to establish and stitch together.

Above: This space's matrix is composed of various sedge species that have knit tightly together in just one year.

Right: A matrix of warm-season bunchgrasses in early summer. Shown are sideoats grama, little bluestem, and indiangrass.

Preparing the Bed

Most folks create a new garden area from one of these scenarios: converting a lawn, updating an established bed, redoing worn-out beds, or working from a blank slate of exposed soil after construction.

The larger and more complex your landscape, the longer your prep time will be. You may need to remove unwanted vegetation, such as trees and shrubs, or deal with invasive plants. However, if you have a weedy lawn, or you're trying to refresh or completely rework older or overrun beds, you'll absolutely have to take a calculated approach for best results. Why? Weeds. Weeds. Weeds.

Even if your lawn is pristine and thick, maintained with fertilizer and preemergents with annual aerating and a compost top dressing, weed seeds are there, just waiting for a chance to feel sunlight. Often, these weeds are mostly annuals, plants that will diminish significantly in years 2 and 3 if not allowed to seed, especially if the bed includes dense, desired plant growth. But during those years of letting weeds go, you may have an unsightly landscape that requires more time to nurture than anticipated, all at the expense of healthy

A 5,000-foot bed is the perfect size to mix plugs and seeding. Masses of forbs were placed directly into the killed lawn in autumn, and a spring sowing of bunchgrasses and annual forbs will follow to provide the matrix and first-year color.

ornamental plants. The more you can do from the start to minimize weeds, the more stable and acceptable your natural garden will be for neighbors.

Many prep options exist, and we will go through the pros and cons of each. Some techniques are more controversial than others, so please keep an open mind, as you'll need to decide what's best for you and your site. In a weedy lawn or other area, a series of efficient spray kills every 4–6 weeks may be ideal, starting in late May and lasting until early fall. This spacing allows weed seeds to exhaust themselves by germinating over and over; spray once seedlings get several inches tall, ensuring they can take the kill more effectively. Doing a late-summer or early-fall kill of a healthy lawn is an ideal situation, as you most likely will have to spray only once and won't have to worry much about weed competition in the fall. You can plant straight into the dead grass and even sow perennials, sedge, and cool-season grasses. The dead lawn acts as both erosion control and a mulch over the winter and into spring, naturally suppressing weeds and adding organic matter.

Using a specific form of herbicide that targets only foliage and quickly breaks down in the soil is critical (don't use a pre-emergent). For many, the ends justify the means on this polarizing subject of strategic chemical use. Keep in mind that there's a significant difference between one-time or minimal use to establish a biodiverse home landscape and corporations with over 200 million acres of monoculture crops (corn, soybeans, wheat) repeatedly applying various synthetic herbicides on chemical-ready, genetically modified plants year after year. Also, glyphosate only targets leaves, stems, and roots by inhibiting amino-acid production. Soil microorganisms then quickly break it down into phosphorous and amino acids, making it far more benign than commonly recommended herbicides like 2,4-D and even organic horticultural vinegar (20 percent acetic acid) which is incredibly caustic. According to studies by the EPA, glyphosate has an environmental impact quotient (EIQ) toxicity rating of 15.3 on a scale of 0–100; some organic pest-control methods, such as insecticidal soap (19), horticultural oil (27.5), and pyrethrin (39) have an even higher EIQ (see Jeff Gilman's *The Truth about Organic Gardening*). Compared with other methods, glyphosate is the most cost effective, reduces soil disturbance better, and is easier on bad backs and sore knees or for those with sudden fatigue syndrome. And life would be much harder on habitat conservationists and restoration managers if they couldn't use it to spot-treat invasive plants or prepare massive areas for high-diversity prairie seeding. It should go without saying that if you use glyphosate, reading the directions—which so many don't do—is important, especially the part on spraying in the correct weather conditions while avoiding use near bodies of water.

Using a sod cutter can be physically demanding, while hidden weed seeds are now exposed for easy germination, but the site prep (and charming legs) are immediate.

Using even a single herbicide just one time, as suggested here, will stir many passions, and recommending its use comes with reservations. For example, I am certainly not an apologist for large chemical corporations that own our food supply and whose deep pockets successfully lobby government officials; the dangers that the wholesale use of their products pose are significant. But to throw the baby out with the bathwater isn't necessarily the best way to go in habitat restoration,

An established garden with gaps filled up by wood mulch is a perfect opportunity to add plant layers and reduce opportunities for weeds to pop up.

where environmental pressures have been exacerbated by human importation of plants and other organisms, not to mention climate change. Managing and mitigating weeds before a garden install is of utmost importance, and minimal site disturbance is key to this prep work.

All that being said, if you are dead set against an herbicide, other methods are available, with their own caveats that you'll need to weigh. You can rent a sod cutter to prep a site in a day, but it is an unwieldy machine that emits harmful exhaust and requires good upper body strength. There's also the issue of what to do with all that sod if you don't have a compost pile, and the exposed bare soil means weed seeds are ready to leap. Solarizing is a second alternative, where you place a black or clear plastic blanket over an area to bake weeds. The strategy here should be to start in May, and after 4–6 weeks, take the cover off for 2 weeks so weeds germinate (you'll need rainfall), then put the cover back on for 4–6 weeks, and repeat. However, solarizing produces a lot of plastic waste and fries soil microbial life.

Another alternative method of site prep is sheet mulching, often with cardboard or newspaper. Sheet or lasagna mulching is very effective, but it's im-

An initial application of 1–2 inches of wood or leaf mulch may be just enough to mitigate some early weed germination before plants take over in subsequent years. Too much mulch, especially in shady areas, will inhibit plants from filling in via runners and seed, since mulch breaks down slower in shade than in sun.

practical for large areas (you'll need lots of cardboard). Some studies have shown that sheet mulching reduces air and water transfer between the soil and atmosphere—essentially, the soil can't breathe. If our goal is to build healthy soil, both solarizing and sheet mulching present trade-offs. Some might recommend double digging, but again, this is impractical for large areas or for those with health issues, plus it causes massive site disturbance that alters the soil profile and exposes weed seeds to sunlight.

Why not just pull weeds if you can stay on top of it after planting? Exactly—if you can stay on top of it. Weeding can take up 90 percent of your management time the first year if you don't plan to mitigate it from the start, plus the desired plants face higher levels of competition above and below the soil line. Most folks pull weeds, which brings new weed seeds to the surface to germinate while leaving a pile of exposed soil for wind-blown seeds to establish in. It's better to deadhead—especially if you're working with annual weeds—either by hand or with a string or hedge trimmer.

Whatever you do, avoid tilling. It's easy to see how it could be ideal—you're ripping out weeds and their roots while amending and aerating soil for planting. But tilling is simply bringing a ton of weed seeds to the surface to germinate, all while destroying the soil structure and profile. Even on a new build with clay soil, tilling to break up compaction or to add organic matter like compost can create problems. It will increase weeds and, in the case of the latter, create a bed that may be too rich for many prairie natives, so they will then perform poorly. Over time, most clay soils will naturally open through freeze-thaw cycles and as various root forms push into the clay—more plants equals more roots equals more soil restoration. The sooner a plant can touch the site's native soil, the better for establishment, resilience, and natural amendment.

Wood mulch is another tool to minimize weeds, but it's not a magical elixir. One or two inches is just enough to inhibit some annual weeds the first year while plants get established and fill in to take over as a living green mulch. Be careful not to put 4, 6, or 12" of mulch on a bed—that will just create an ideal layer for weeds to germinate while inhibiting water from reaching deep down into the soil. And of course, you can't seed into wood mulch.

Ultimately, your method of prep is a personal choice based on a host of variables such as garden design method, management ability, scale, and cost—but your goal should always be to minimize site disturbance, for the benefit of soil life, soil structure, and mitigating weed germination that may compete with desired plants.

Changing Expectations

Perhaps one of the larger hurdles for folks new to nature-based gardening is in the length of establishment and the style of management (a.k.a. not helicopter gardening). It's probably safe to say that if you are reading this book, you

Letting plants find their way and not helicopter parenting is a core management strategy in natural gardens.

Also, learning to see leaf damage as desirable is an important hurdle to overcome. These silvery checkerspot larvae are enjoying black-eyed Susans.

understand gardens take time to develop and fill in. This is especially true when you are using cost-effective plugs and seed, as well as smaller trees that will establish faster and soon catch up to larger, stress-prone specimens that cost a small fortune.

I have new clients sign an expectations agreement in which I lay out how the garden will develop, and how we'll need to manage it in ways that differ from what they may be used to. I find this transparency sets up more realistic expectations and even involves more long-term collaboration between us as partners in a process, learning as a team about the plants and how each site is unique. So what are some of these expectations?

- Plants take several years to establish. Some plants won't flower for 2–4 years while they are growing their roots.
- This garden is unlike traditional gardens. Plants will move, self-sow, spread, and die as a natural process. This garden is designed to replicate the aforementioned natural processes and change over time.
- In a natural garden, plants are meant to stand in winter to protect their crowns and increase soil moisture, among other ecosystem services such as wildlife habitat. Therefore, plants should remain standing in winter to mimic natural processes, and fallen leaves should remain to add soil nutrients and provide shelter.
- Overwatering kills plants as easily as underwatering. When plants are matched to the site, they will not need supplemental watering after establishment.
- No fertilizer or pesticides should be used at any time.

Early Management

In traditional gardening, the mantra is water, fertilize, mulch, water, weed, water, mulch, water. In more natural gardening, the mantra is more like: plants, water, weed, more plants, let the plants find their way, lightly edit, relax. If herbivore damage is a concern, it's important to note that fertilizing increases the nitrogen content of leaves, making them tastier, and too much irrigation promotes succulent new growth. As a garden designer, I'm hesitant to offer blanket advice

Plant density is critical, whether that's using all plugs or a combination of plugs and seed. First-year clipping, trimming, or mowing of weed flowers also helps to ensure there are fewer issues in subsequent years.

on management because every site is so different, and weather is a significant variable. That being said, since we've already explored general advice on plant selection, designing, and planting, let's do the same for initial management.

Year 1

In the first 2–4 weeks after planting, water 1–2 times a week. Each plug should directly receive 10 seconds of a medium amount of spray (not a mist, not a jet wash) twice a week. Spring and summer planting will require more watering and constant monitoring until fall, whereas fall plantings may require less watering or none at all. For larger areas, sprinklers are best and will likely need to be run for several hours at a time (if you have limited access to water, this may not be as practical as spot watering). You'll tend to water less in clay soils and more in loam or sandy / rocky soils; the latter dry out faster, especially in sun.

Seeded meadows or prairies will benefit from constant, soil-surface moisture the first 2–4 weeks after a spring seeding, and deep watering every 1–2 weeks in the absence of frequent rainfall (deep watering encourages rooting). Using a lightly sown nurse crop or erosion control blanket can help conserve soil moisture for fragile new seedlings on exposed sites.

Every spring after the first growing season will require a mowing or string trimming of plant material. Remove the dead vegetation from dense meadows if you can, to help light reach seeds on the soil surface. Otherwise, in foundation beds, leave the material to act as a mulch layer that quickly degrades.

In spring, leave spent perennial stalks 12–18 inches tall in some areas, which provides habitat for fauna like this small male carpenter bee (*Ceratina*), who may be looking for a mate. Joe pye weed (*Eutrochium* spp.) has hollow stems that are ideal, but plants like coneflowers (*Echinacea* spp.) do well, too, as the bees excavate the pith.

Spring plantings will have to compete with annual weeds. A 1–2" thin mulch layer (if not seeding a matrix) may help. Don't pull weeds unless they are perennials; instead, deadhead flowers and seed heads to reduce soil disturbance. Weed every 2 weeks. Weed pressure will diminish significantly by September. Fall plantings will not see much weed pressure at all, but they may need weed management the following spring and early summer.

If the bed was planted with potted material, hand weeding is necessary. If it was sown, a mower set at 4–6" can be used every 2–3 weeks during the subsequent growing season to ensure weeds don't set seed. Germinating prairie plants won't be affected while they work on root growth. Stop mowing in late summer to early fall, depending on your latitude.

Year 2

A March mow or trim won't be necessary. That's needed only in year 3 and beyond, at which point you can mow the space at 4–6", or better yet for less grass-dominated designs, use a hedge trimmer or weed whacker and cut everything down to about 12", leaving the detritus in place. Burning in some years would be ideal, but it's often illegal within city limits.

During the second summer, plants will fill in, and weed pressure should have dropped to the point where a quick walk will take care of most issues. Some weeds may even be unnoticeable or not worth the effort as they are quickly outcompeted by grasses, sedge, and biennials. In 100-percent seeded gardens, you may need to do a few high mowings or use a string trimmer; generally, cutting at 12" is best. Do an occasional deep watering only if there's a prolonged drought.

Some plants may need to be replaced. If the space was seeded, a spring / early summer seeding of grass may be needed, as well as a fall overseeding of perennial forbs. More on seeding and management can be found in the next chapter.

DEER- AND RABBIT-TOLERANT FORBS

While herbivore pressure can vary based on a host of environmental and population conditions, the below selection of herbaceous perennials show general resistance to herbivory. To reduce browsing of treasured plants, try surrounding them with plants deer and rabbits don't enjoy—like plant bodyguards.

Rattlesnake master (*Eryngium yuccifolium*)
Anise hyssop (*Agastache foeniculum*)
Aromatic aster (*Symphyotrichum oblongifolium*)
Sedge (*Carex* spp.)
Little bluestem (*Schizachyrium scoparium*)
Sideoats grama (*Bouteloua curtipendula*)
Nodding onion (*Allium cernuum*)
Mountain mint (*Pycnanthemum* spp.)
Arkansas bluestar (*Amsonia hubrichtii*)
Ironweed (*Vernonia* spp.)
Tall thimbleweed (*Anemone virginiana*)
Goldenrod (*Solidago* spp., *Oligoneuron* spp.)
Wild bergamot (*Monarda fistulosa*)

Nodding onion (*Allium cernuum*) does well intermingled among shortgrasses, and it won't be eaten by rabbits.

Western spiderwort (*Tradescantia occidentalis*)
Golden Alexanders (*Zizia aurea*)
Switchgrass (*Panicum virgatum*)
Wild ginger (*Asarum canadense*)
Black-eyed Susan (*Rudbeckia hirta*)
Tickseed (*Coreopsis* spp.)
Blue sage (*Salvia azurea*)
Sneezeweed (*Helenium autumnale*)

A Note on Letting Plants Find Their Way

Our goal is always to put the right plant in with the right plant communities. Even in a hybrid, designed approach, where ornamental layers are placed purposefully with plugs, and a green mulch of grass is sown in, the fact that plants are dynamic and not static will soon become evident. It's our ability to embrace that dynamism and competition that sets natural gardens apart from their traditional counterparts.

In a smaller garden, we'd be wise to choose plants that are generally behaved clumpers—they won't spread too much by runners or sowing. But site conditions can affect these plants, as clay soil and dense, layered vegetation generally will inhibit plant reproduction, while loamy or sandy soil with less plant competition generally will encourage it. If most of the plants that are best suited to your site tend to have aggressive natures, it's best to use *all* aggressive plant species so they butt heads, collide, and help keep each other in check. And do keep in mind this understanding: the difference between aggressive and invasive is the difference between a native plant filling its niche and an exotic plant altering an ecosystem to produce a monoculture.

In a new garden, we also shouldn't place plugs or 2" pots based on their mature size. If a plant tag, or thorough internet and book research, shows that a full-grown plant gets 3' wide, we should still plant it 12" from its neighbor. Why would you do that, especially when plants cost money and losing even one can be like a shot to the heart? Because our goal is to cover the ground ASAP, preferably in the first year and definitely by summer of the second year. Place your plants based on size at the time of installation; over time, the more robust species and specimens will outcompete the lesser ones, and that's OK as long as the ground stays covered in the future.

Once those plants get going and are competing healthily, it's time to crack open a hard lemonade. You can crack open another one when you start seeing plants move around and find their own way—which is exactly what you want as they fill in, create layers, and augment the design you kick-started. You can always thin and transplant—that's what gardeners do—but you'll be surprised and even thankful at what the plants teach as they shuffle, thrive, and falter. Let that dynamic purpose have its way, especially since you planned for it by using multiple layers and plants suited for the site. You've also planned for plants to fill niches—layers of succession and layers of seasonality, as well as layers in time.

An urban shade garden filled with various sedge species provides an effective green-mulch matrix and myriad ecosystem services.

Let's further consider *Rudbeckia hirta*, a freely self-sowing biennial that often is the scourge of the garden as it seeks to create a monoculture. However, you can be a Rudbeckia whisperer. Black-eyed Susan has first-year basal foliage that is well-suited to erosion control and shading out weed seeds in the soil surface. You'll even get a few first-year flowers to appease neighbors and bees. In the second year, the fuller flower flush will appear alongside some of the early-establishing perennials, and in year three—once the perennials have really started to fill in—the Rudbeckia seeds will have less light in which to germinate. If you seeded in a bunchgrass matrix, the grasses will allow the black-eyed Susan to create charming little stands or solitary spikes of flowers, in balance with the competition provided by the grasses.

One final strategy to consider when using a matrix is based on how grasses tend to dominate in both a prairie and a garden. In some ways, we want lots of grasses, as they are effective at erosion and weed control while providing critical wildlife habitat. Still, we obviously want flowers (and so do pollinators,

A mix of annual and biennial forbs helps add color and weed suppression to any size meadow planting in its early years. By year three, these plants at Bellevue University will fade as perennials and grasses take over. Pictured are: plains coreopsis (*Coreopsis tinctoria*), clasping coneflower (*Dracopis amplexicaulis*), and Mexican hat coneflower (*Ratibida columnifera*). © Tyler Moore. Used with permission.

Black-eyed Susan (*Rudbeckia hirta*) is a favorite among pollen-seeking bees, as this crab spider can attest.

On some projects, it's not possible to pluck out every weed. Here, black-eyed Susan and other species are competing against (and even working with) annual weeds while rebuilding the site in the first growing season. Sometimes, weeds can blend in and look natural.

spiders, and birds). When choosing forbs, consider selecting plants that spread by rhizome or root runners, or that have taproots or corms, as well as those that tend to produce good amounts of seed. That last point is counterintuitive to what we explored earlier, about not using free-seeding flowers in a small bed; and that still holds true for a small bed. But in larger areas approaching several thousand square feet, we want to have at least a few plants that cast their seed around—and maybe we especially want those that drop seed near the mother plant to create larger colonies, masses, and drifts.

You can see there's a lot to consider, but I wouldn't want to do without at least 50 percent grass cover because of its many benefits to ecosystem function. If you find grasses starting to tip the balance too much, say 70 percent, management like early-summer mowing, dormant forb overseeding, and definitely planting more plugs in fall will turn the tide.

COMMON FIRST-YEAR WEEDS

These are some of the most likely unwanted plants you'll see popping up in a new bed, especially during the growing season. An internet search of the scientific name will help you learn how, or even whether, you need to control the weed. Do note that some of these are edible.

Henbit (*Lamium amplexicaule*)
Purple deadnettle (*Lamium purpureum*)
Crabgrass (*Digitaria sanguinalis*)
Prickly lettuce (*Lactuca serriola*)
Yellow, green, or giant foxtail (*Setaria* spp.)
Barnyard grass (*Echinochola crus-galli*)
Yellow nutsedge (*Cyperus esculentus*)
Siberian elm (*Ulmus pumila*)
Quackgrass (*Elymus repens*)
Marestail (*Erigeron canadensis*)
Black medic (*Medicago lupulina*)
Lambsquarter (*Chenopodium album*)
Purslane (*Portulaca oleracea*)
Ragweed (*Ambrosia* spp.)

Successes and Failures

It bears repeating that no two gardens are the same, even when the same plants and methods have been used. Every site presents different unseen challenges and opportunities, while natural factors such as weather create an unpredictability that is both frustrating and part of the joyful equation of allowing an ecosystem to find its way and teach you, too.

None of us is ever going to be an expert at gardening. Sure, our confidence will grow with experience, and we'll likely know more than many, but gardening is not like building a house or a car or a lamp. Those processes always have specific parameters to follow that produce precise outcomes. A garden is not perfect on the day it's installed, and it will require management, care, and fine-tuning that we need to anticipate and plan for. We can only hope to get close with our parameters, and our outcomes will always need to be malleable. After all, we are working with living, even sentient beings in a complex web we barely understand, ultimately.

I've had my share of lucky gardens and those that required more intensive tweaking, and a brief look at some hiccups may help you along. One of the earliest gardens I designed used *Carex brevior* as a green mulch; it's very adaptable and looks great the first season—low and even a little poofy. But in year 2, it does what all *C. brevior* does by getting 3' tall and then flopping over. It not only looks unsightly but also smothers other plants. I eventually decided to have the client cut back the sedge by 50 percent around June 1 of every year.

You can hedge your bets on problem sites that need faster coverage by using layers of aggressive species that collide and interlock together. Shown here are pearly everlasting (*Anaphalis margaritacea*), purple poppy mallow (*Callirhoe involucrata*), dense blazingstar (*Liatris spicata*), shrubby St. John's wort (*Hypericum prolificum*), and little bluestem, among others. © Prairie Moon Nursery. Used with permission.

If I had to do it all over again, I'd have sown in some low bunchgrasses or gone with a different sedge species, like clustered field sedge (*Carex praegracilis*).

A second garden I was able to pivot on a bit faster—a large space we planted with forbs and then sowed with grasses in autumn. The lesson on this project was to go ahead and sow warm-season grasses in fall, but come back and do it again in spring. I'm not sure whether even doubling the rate in fall would have made a difference, because spring sowing is just so much better at high germination. This mini prairie was sown and planted into a killed lawn and not roughed in, allowing for the winter freeze-thaw cycle to incorporate the seeds. We had poor grass germination even into June, at which point weeds were having a field day. I came back with a late-spring sowing of prairie grasses, and while they are not as robust as another area where I simply sowed grasses in early to mid-May, it contains plenty of grass seedlings, so I know the next growing season will be markedly improved.

Finally, a much larger backyard was sown in early January, which may have been too late to get some forb seeds to break dormancy, because it ended up being a mild second half of winter. Further, we did not do a regimen of weed killing the growing season before, mostly because it was a new build that was pretty bare. In hindsight, the best method would have been to do a summer of weed mitigation and then sow in October; however, with overseeding and constant mowing at 6" high the first year, we're slowly catching up.

A small bed that receives a few hours of midday sun is being overrun by penn sedge (*Carex pensylvanica*) and seedlings of purple coneflower (*Echinacea purpurea*). Or is it a happy, spontaneous, self-organizing ecosystem that's creating what the site needs?

While these might seem like minor issues that will always occur, the nuances of each project keep me honest and fairly humble—you never quite know what you're going to get, but you know you'll have to stay on top of the garden the first 1–3 years and be flexible. Still, I'd rather have the garden look like what's in my head a month after planting and to do so flawlessly; even garden designers are prone to delusions of grandeur and impatience, I suppose.

Thistles aren't a problem unless they're musk or Canada thistle. Our native thistles, like this *Cirsium altissimum*, are incredibly beneficial.

Monarchs love to nectar on *Liatris ligulistylis*, which is sometimes mistaken for a thistle species, but meadow voles also love to devour the corms over winter. The happy compromise is to plant a ton of blazingstar.

It's easy to shy away from tall coreopis (*C. tripteris*) because of its moderate root runners and height of 6–8 feet. But as we experiment and learn about plants, tall coreopsis teaches us about cadence, purpose, and community. The stems are open and airy, the bloom time is long in late summer when many pollinators are active, and it turns a lovely yellow in autumn with decent winter interest.

A natural garden can show just as much design intention and textural beauty in fall and winter, not to mention a continuation of ecosystem services.

4

DESIGNING THE GARDEN

"Designers can stylize natural distribution in several ways. The simplest way is to create tighter, denser, and larger versions of the patterns than those in the wild. Example: if wild aster forms loose drifts through a field of grasses, then perhaps these drifts are represented by a thicker mass of asters in a designed planting. Or if a *Liatris spicata* dots itself singly through a prairie, perhaps a designed planting would use clusters of five or seven plants to create a more robust, readable version than what happens in the wild. To achieve the same effect in a smaller garden, we have to use more of the same at higher density."

—THOMAS RAINER AND CLAUDIA WEST

It's time to get down to business. And you're ready. This practical chapter focuses on two methods of installing a garden—seeding and planting—as well as a hybrid approach between the two. Different situations call for different methods, but knowing as much as you can about the two approaches will help you design and manage the garden for various goals. For example, knowing how seed from various plant species germinates will help you design a garden with plugs and anticipate succession as plants mature and create a community.

Seeding

Let's start with what is as fine an art as using potted plants, and which is not as simple as it may seem. In fact, with seeding, just like with using potted plants, the lessons never end, and mastery is a tantalizing carrot on a stick. With seeding, the site analysis, prep, install, and even management can be different from planting a garden with plugs. You also have to understand whether the seed needs to be buried and at what depth, as well as when to sow which species and at what rates. Sometimes the seed mix will be simple because the space is small and can be tended easily, including watering, weeding, thinning, and overseeding. However, in a larger space where intense management may be less practical, diversity will be critical to create a self-maintaining ecosystem where plants fit every niche. As Travis Beck says: "The designer's art in diverse communities is not to set the exact proportions and blends of different plants but to create a mix of plants that can respond dynamically to changing conditions." While this statement is true for planted spaces, it's doubly true for seeded landscapes, where plants take longer to establish, and thus the space has more windows for drought, deluges, and weeds to affect establishment.

Dwarf red plains coreopsis (*Coreopsis tinctoria*) is an annual that performs as a gap filler of first-year color in a new garden.

In a diverse seeding, you want to have a variety of species acting in different roles: early successional / pioneers that cover the ground and get blooming quickly; legumes that fix nitrogen; warm-season and cool-season grasses that create a matrix base from spring to fall; annuals for first-year green mulch and color; and perennials that take a bit longer to get going but may also be longer-lived and more stable. These functions expand on the basic principles outlined earlier in plant selection for a designed garden bed, such as bloom color and time, form, habit, reproduction, and ecosystem services.

The design possibilities are endless when you combine seeding and planting. This image shows how a little restraint in the forb layer increases legibility without sacrificing color and pollinator resources. © Dan Carter. Used with permission.

Seeding requires greater knowledge in other areas, as well, especially understanding seed mix percentages and germination rates. Some species germinate easily once spring and early-summer warmth hit. Others need periods of stratification that may require a few weeks or months of cold, damp winter weather, or even several seasons and years, to break dormancy. The rate at which species can break dormancy and create a seedling may be specific to not only ecotype but also ecoregion, as well as weather and site conditions like soil and available light. I've read many books and even cataloged germination rates to estimate how well a species will go from seed to seedling, but variables always throw a wrench into the plans, leading me to see the benefits of seeding at high rates.

In this chapter, you'll get a basic understanding of what it takes to choose seeds, at what rates to sow in what conditions, and which species may be the safest bets for reliable development. Keep in mind, though, these basic guidelines are no substitute for research in your ecoregion and talking with local experts—they are simply a jumping-off point for experimentation, which is gardening 101.

Seed Selection

In general, here's what you need to consider when choosing seeds to create a custom mix tailored to your site and ecosystem goals:

- Site conditions (not only what we've covered earlier regarding soil, light, and other factors, but also whether you will be seeding into bare ground or killed sod, as that affects seeding rates).
- Plant sociability, behavior, and lifespan
- Bloom time
- Early successional / pioneer, warm- or cool-season grass, legume, perennial or annual
- Germination code

Shade gardens can be as diverse and as lush as their full-sun relatives, even when using a strictly native plant palette. © Dan Carter. Used with permission.

- Seed planting depth
- Germination rate percentage of pure live seed, or PLS (any reputable seed producer can supply these)
- Seeds per ounce of each species
- PLS weight and bulk weight per ounce
- Seeding rate (this is often calculated by germination rates and / or cost)

The path of least resistance to creating a sown meadow bed is to prepare a space with bare soil, use a seed mix designed for your site conditions from a reputable native plant nursery or seed farm, hand broadcast in late autumn or early winter, let snow and rain work seed into soil, then see what happens in spring. This approach may or may not provide the intended results, but there are ways to get closer to ensure seed germination. If you want to increase chances of success, you could put down a straw erosion control blanket (ECB) over your bed or employ a nurse crop like oats, rye, or winter wheat—two strategies that will help keep soil moist and seeds protected.

You could also sow species that need cold, moist stratification in late autumn, and then come back in mid- to late spring and sow in warm-season grasses, annuals, and those perennials with germination code A (which means they need no stratification). But perhaps the best way to ensure success is to create a tailored seed mix, in which every seed is suited to your site, aesthetic, and ecological goals.

In a part-shade site, take advantage of plants that give you more plants, like hairy wood mint (*Blephilia hirsuta*) that spreads by rhizomes, and tall bellflower (*Campanula americana*), which is a self-sowing biennial that pokes up through other plants. © Prairie Moon Nursery. Used with permission.

GERMINATION CODES

Every native plant species has a corresponding code to let you know what environmental conditions it requires to break dormancy and germinate. This knowledge will help you time seeding and plan for succession. Here are some of the most common germination codes.

A–Seed will germinate when sown in a warm location; no pre-treatment needed, but should be stored in a cold, dry area over winter.
B–Needs boiling water poured over it and should soak for 24 hours.
C–Seed requires X number of days in cold, moist conditions (for example, C10, C30, C60).
D–Very small seeds that should be surface-sown.
E–Seeds need a warm, moist period (80°F) followed by a cold, moist period (33–38°F) of 60–90 days each.
F–These hardy seeds require a cold period followed by a warm period, followed by another cold period.
G–Seeds benefit from late-fall sowing after a hard frost.
H–These seeds have hard outer shells that, if sown in spring, need to be scarified or roughed up. Fall-sown seeds should not be scarified.

Most milkweed, like this part-shade purple milkweed (*Asclepias purpurascens*), require at least 30 days of cold, moist conditions before their seed can germinate.

On the other hand, culver's root (*Veronicastrum virginicum*) has very small seeds that must be surface-sown after the danger of frost has passed in spring.

Creating a Custom Seed Mix

You've studied up on plants and you've found a local seed supplier that's listed its crop availability. You have a budget, you know your site, and you know your ecosystem function and aesthetic goals. Now let's say you have 2,000 square feet you'd like to sow. Generally speaking, a prairie-style seeding has the following ratios:

50 seeds / ft.
50 percent grass (25 seeds / ft.)
50 percent forbs (25 seeds / ft.)

Some gardeners may prefer to start out with more flowers first, while others may want to increase grasses because their site is prone to erosion or aggressive weeds, and they need a dominant, stabilizing cover ASAP.

With our 50 / 50 mix, let's break the percentages down further into functional groups, as we did similarly in chapter 2 for plugs:

35 percent warm-season grass
15 percent cool-season grass and / or sedge
10 percent legumes
10 percent annuals
30 percent perennials

Why are we using these percentages? While some site and / or aesthetic goals will require different percentages, this is generally a solid breakdown to hit as many goals as possible at one time. The warm-season grasses will do the bulk of the matrix work, while the cool-season grasses and sedge will

Tools of the seed-mixing trade: a concrete floor, tarp, bucket, and scale. Plastic or paper baggies are another necessity.

The beauty and promise of the seed mix is a tantalizing hors d'oeuvre to what will follow in the coming years. If you can identify these seeds, you deserve a prize.

Asters tend to self-sow easily, so plan for this reality in your seed mix calculations (for example, you may want more or fewer aster species).

help with weed control and site stabilization in the shoulder seasons when they grow most actively. Legumes add nitrogen to the soil, while annuals provide first-year weed competition, erosion control, and color. Perennial flowers will do the bulk of the aesthetic show, and within their 30 percent is a mix of early successional species as well as those that take longer to establish but that are also longer lived. Now, let's take a look at a sample list and seed weights; do note that this is a very basic list using illustrative species and is not necessarily meant for application.

The Seeds

Since you'll be buying seed by the ounce, you'll need to know how many seeds are in an ounce; that information can be found most easily online at Prairie Moon Nursery for each species you're using. Then it's simple math. For example, *Echinacea pallida* has 5,200 seeds per ounce, so if you have a 2,000' bed, you'll need just less than 1/2 oz. to get one seed per foot. *Rudbeckia hirta* has 92,000 seeds per ounce, so for that same bed, you'll need 0.03 oz. (just a small packet). Let's get to that proposed seed list.

CALCULATING SEEDS PER FOOT

Sample calculation for sideoats grama (*Bouteloua curtipendula*), assuming it alone would comprise the warm-season grass percentage of a seeded area:

50 seeds per foot x 0.35 (35 percent) = 17 seeds per foot
17 seeds per foot x 2,000 square feet = 34,000 seeds
34,000 seeds / 6,600 seeds per ounce = 5.15 oz

Seed List

2,000' area at 50 seeds per foot on bare soil:

35 percent warm-season grass (17 seeds/ft.)

Bouteloua curtipendula
6,600 seeds per ounce, 17 seeds per foot, 34,000 seeds = 5.15 oz.

15 percent cool-season grass / sedge (8 seeds/ft.)

Carex brevior
29,000 seeds per ounce, 4 seeds per foot, 8,000 seeds = 0.28 oz.

Carex rosea
53,000 seeds per ounce, 4 seeds per foot, 8,000 seeds = 0.15 oz.

10 percent legumes (6 seeds/ft.)

Amorpha canescens
16,000 seeds per ounce, 3 seeds per foot, 6,000 seeds = 0.375 oz.

Dalea purpurea
15,000 seeds per ounce, 3 seeds per foot, 6,000 seeds = 0.375 oz.

10 percent annuals (6 seeds/ft.)

Coreopsis tinctoria
87,500 seeds per ounce, 3 seeds per foot, 6,000 seeds = 0.069 oz.

Chamaecrista fasciculata
2,700 seeds per ounce, 3 seeds per foot, 6,000 seeds = 2.2 oz.

30 percent perennials (15 seeds/ft.)

Zizia aurea
11,000 seeds per ounce, 2 seeds per foot, 4,000 seeds = 0.36 oz.

Echinacea pallida
5,200 seeds per ounce, 2 seeds per foot, 4,000 seeds = 0.77 oz.

Asclepias tuberosa
4,300 seeds per ounce, 2 seeds per foot, 4,000 seeds = 0.93 oz.

Pycnanthemum tenuifolium
378,000 seeds per ounce, 2 seeds per foot, 4,000 seeds = 0.01 oz.

Rudbeckia hirta
92,000 seeds per ounce, 2 seeds per foot, 4,000 seeds = 0.043 oz.

Liatris aspera
16,000 seeds per ounce, 2 seeds per foot, 4,000 seeds = 0.25 oz.

Ratibida pinnata
30,000 seeds per ounce, 2 seeds per foot, 4,000 seeds = 0.13 oz.

Symphyotrichum laeve
55,000 seeds per ounce, 2 seeds per foot, 4,000 seeds = 0.07 oz.

Total weight of pure live seed = 11.162 oz.

This basic custom seed mix is not without its issues. For example, Liatris species are notoriously poor at germinating, so you might want to increase their seeding rate (or plant plugs), but at the same time, most Liatris species are also expensive as seed. Another issue is that Pycnanthemum has very small seeds and can easily germinate with a spring sowing—so maybe it's best not to sow this one in fall or winter. Some species may germinate easily, grow fast, and produce copious amounts of seed, so you might want to use less of those. Each species will present little quirks like this, and if you want to research germina-

Golden Alexanders (*Zizia aurea*) and white wild indigo (*Baptisia alba*) provide two different bloom structures to help a wide variety of spring pollinators. © Prairie Moon Nursery. Used with permission.

Hoary vervain (*Verbena stricta*) might seem weedy on roadside margins, but in a lush, layered garden, it's fairly behaved. Some 140 insect species have been observed using hoary vervain.

tion rates, go right ahead; however, the best thing to do is to increase your species diversity. You might want to double the perennial forb species, which would mean more potential resilience and ecosystem services. For example, perhaps add more species in the aster family.

There's probably not a magic bullet for creating a custom seed mix. Generally, I'm trying to give you a middle-of-the road baseline that you can tweak. While warm-season grass seed may do best with a late-spring seeding, it also might not be practical, which is why doubling its rate in a dormant seeding

Wild quinine (*Parthenium integrifolium*) is underplanted. Cauliflower-like blooms give way to a winter-long seed head display.

may be a good idea. Seeds of any plant type can be eaten or washed away, or they just never do anything, so I subscribe to the more-is-better-if-you-can-afford-it approach. When you buy seed, you should see a tag showing PLS (pure live seed); this percentage is calculated by taking into consideration seed purity, germination rate, and seed dormancy. You can use PLS to increase or decrease rates of each species based on the expected germination rate. See, it gets quite complex, and if it's too much for you right now, just know that the most important aspect in a seeding is diversity—diversity of species, niches, and ecosystem function so you create resilience.

In the end, we simply want to cover the ground ASAP and we want competition ASAP; the more plants we have with a diversity of functional groups, the sooner a garden can perform ecosystem services. Several studies of prairie restorations show that the ratio of survival from seed to mature plant is generally around 5–10 percent, so if you want 5 plants per square foot, you'll need to sow 50 seeds per square foot.

AFFORDABLE FLOWER SEED

In general, these are often some of the most affordable sun-loving forb seeds, perennial and biennial, generally near or under $10 per ounce as of this writing:

Golden Alexanders (*Zizia aurea*)
Foxglove beardtongue (*Penstemon digitalis*)
Black-eyed Susan (*Rudbeckia hirta*)
Upright or Mexican hat coneflower (*Ratibida columnifera*)
Purple prairie clover (*Dalea purpurea*)
Shrubby St. John's wort (*Hypericum prolificum*)
Canada milkvetch (*Astragalus canadensis*)
Bundleflower (*Desmanthus illinoensis*)
Purple coneflower (*Echinacea purpurea*)
Rattlesnake master (*Eryngium yuccifolium*)
Hoary vervain (*Verbena stricta*)
Common evening primrose (*Oenothera biennis*)
Blue vervain (*Verbena hastata*)
Wild quinine (*Parthenium integrifolium*)
Lanceleaf coreopsis (*Coreopsis lanceolata*)
Prairie blazingstar (*Liatris pycnostachya*)
Early / oxeye sunflower (*Heliopsis helianthoides*)
Cup plant (*Silphium perfoliatum*)
Stiff goldenrod (*Oligoneuron rigidum*)

Seeding Rates

Your seeding rate will change based on various factors, including site conditions and desired outcomes. At minimum, you'll always want to sow 50 seeds per foot, but there are reasons to adjust that number.

You'll want to increase seeds per square foot by about 50 percent for slopes, and ensure you at least use an ECB or nurse crop to keep seeds in place. If you're sowing into spray-killed lawn, a 100 percent increase in seeds per foot is a good idea—so 50 seeds per foot becomes 100—while the dead lawn may be able to fill the role of an ECB or nurse crop.

I prefer the laziest method possible that disturbs the site as little as possible. That's why, just as in using plugs, it's not ideal to till soil unless it's super-hardpan clay that a screwdriver can't penetrate a few inches down when moistened.

A specialist native bee, the beebalm shortface (*Dufourea monardae*) relies on the pollen of wild bergamot; the perennial's small seeds are best surface-sown in spring or summer.

One of the few plants you can hear from twenty feet away, wild senna (*Senna hebecarpa*) is often filled with foraging worker bumble bees that buzz-pollinate the blooms with great vigor.

If you're working with a large area that is quite weedy, you'll want to start a regimen of spray killing (or whatever method you'd like to use) in late spring all the way into fall to exhaust weeds, always letting weed seeds germinate repeatedly only to knock them back again. If you have pristine lawn, spray kill it in late August to early September, depending on latitude. Let the grass grow long to 6" in midsummer so it can take the chemical more easily. Broadcast sow at 100–125 seeds per foot (you can create a mix for 50 seeds per foot, then double or triple the per-species weight) to account for slightly lower germination rates in dead lawns.

SEED THAT GERMINATES READILY IN LATE SPRING AND SUMMER

These species require no pre-treatment (code A) and are ideally suited for sites with medium to dry soils in full to part sun.

Perennials and Grasses:

- Sideoats grama (*Bouteloua curtipendula*)
- Little bluestem (*Schizachyrium scoparium*)
- White prairie clover (*Dalea candida*)
- Purple prairie clover (*Dalea purpurea*)
- Purple coneflower (*Echinacea purpurea*)
- Sneezeweed (*Helenium autumnale*)
- Shrubby St. John's wort (*Hypericum prolificum*)
- Wild bergamot (*Monarda fistulosa*)
- Slender mountain mint (*Pycnanthemum tenuifolium*)
- Blue sage (*Salvia azurea*)
- Wild senna (*Senna hebecarpa*)
- Maryland senna (*Senna marilandica*)
- Heath aster (*Symphyotrichum ericoides*)
- Smooth aster (*Symphyotrichum laeve*)
- Azure aster (*Symphyotrichum oolentangiense*)

Annuals:

- Partridge pea (*Chamaecrista fasciculata*)
- Rocky Mountain beeplant (*Cleome serrulata*)
- Clasping coneflower (*Dracopis amplexicaulis*)
- Plains coreopsis (*Coreopsis tinctoria*)
- Indian blanket (*Gaillardia pulchella*)

A Note on Hand-Broadcasting Seed

A person can do one acre tossing seed by hand in under a day, and most people reading this book probably won't be sowing anywhere near this size. If you have 5+ acres, you should find a contractor that can use a drop spreader or seed drill—and knows how to calibrate those machines for a wide diversity of prairie seed.

To get a more uniform seed distribution when hand-sowing, you'll want to use a very slightly moistened or dry seed carrier, a medium that bulks up the mix. Most folks use compost, sand, sawdust, or vermiculite at a rate of 0.5 cubic feet (3.75 gallons) per 1,000 square feet. However, for small areas, you can eyeball it—one handful of seed per five handfuls of carrier. I prefer vermiculite, which isn't heavy like sand or compost and, to my eye, provides the most even seed

Don't cut your garden down in fall, part 1: many bird species forage for seed all winter long atop stems and on the ground.

Don't cut your garden down in fall, part 2: let the plants self-sow, and fill in the beds, creating more layers, increasing ecosystem function, and giving you free seedlings to transplant

distribution with the carrier (you can also see where your seed has landed very easily—broadcasting on top of puffy snow that does not have a surface layer of ice on a sunny day also works well). You do not want to hand-broadcast on a windy day—generally, less than 10 mph is good, and 0 is best. Walking with the wind to your back is also helpful, because a light breeze can help carry the seed forward as you broadcast.

If you have a larger space, divide your planting area into 1,000' chunks, then your mix into even amounts for each 1,000' area (a scale helps here). Then divide the seed in two for each 1,000' area. With the first half of seed, walk in one direction back and forth in even rows (usually, a person can do about 4–6' widths), then take the other half of your mix and walk in perpendicular rows. Sow like you live in sparse times—it's better to have leftover mix to do touch-ups than to run out early on your passes.

Management

Managing a sown meadow early on is different from managing a garden full of plugs, even if that garden has a sown matrix of grasses instead of wood mulch. Generally, you'll want to mow the space at 4–6" high all summer long as weeds reach 6–12" in height, making sure to remove the material (if you can) to increase light penetrating to the soil. As in a plugged bed, your biggest weed battle will be with annuals.

Overseeding is best done in the first two years. Like gardening with plugs, the space's development is a process you'll need to guide, and with establishment from seed, the garden takes longer to mature—sometimes 2–3 times as long. A year after an initial dormant seeding is a good time to tweak with another, lighter dormant seeding, and the first spring and summer are also ideal for adding grasses and annuals.

Planting Plans

The goal of this chapter is to start you out on experimentation with the design and management techniques of this book, as well as to introduce you to some resilient native plants in combinations that work together for specific site conditions. Now that we've looked at seeding, we can glimpse how that information broadens the knowledge needed to choose potted plants and create an ecological design that is even more tailored as a garden.

You are encouraged to use plugs or 2" pots, as these sizes give you more bang for your buck, and smaller plants tend to have less transplant shock and establish quickly. If you have a 100' garden and need 50 plants, the per-plant cost for plugs and 2" pots is roughly $2–4. Comparatively, quarts may run you $5–10 and gallons roughly $15. To break that down on a total-cost continuum on the high end, it's $200 vs. $500 vs. $750.

In general, the following plans are based on all that we've learned so far, and they attempt to bridge wild and manicured aesthetics by employing designed masses and

As the years pass, plants will self-organize based on your original arrangement, creating surprising communities that make the garden seem new every season. Let them lead the way.

drifts, while also allowing plants to find their way over time with a light guiding hand. Species are selected based on size and habit, as well as how they will interact over the first 3–5 years. So these are plans you are meant to employ immediately. You'll note that most plants list a specialist insect (often one of many), either an adult bee or butterfly / moth larva; these insects may depend on that particular plant species, genus, or family, and they may or may not be endemic to your ecoregion.

Finally, don't take these plans literally—they are more reference points for creative liberties that are finely tuned to your site. Plans always change once plants are laid out on the ground; in fact, on most projects, I don't even have a formal plan. The best advice may be to take the suggested numbers of each species (plus some extras) and play around in the moment, in the space. Just be sure to keep in mind some basic principles: the plant's social behavior, when it blooms, and its projected mature size. Over time, you'll be able to go further after you observe the plants in your landscape: texture, wildlife support, winter interest, response to other nearby plants, and more.

WHY DO MANY NATIVE PLANTS GET TOO TALL AND FLOP OVER?

1. The soil is too rich. For example, a lot of our prairie and meadow plants evolved in leaner soil conditions like clay. There's often no need to amend if you match plants to the site.
2. There's less competition for resources, above and below ground, so plants can cut loose.
3. An extension of #2–if plants are spread farther apart, there's less buttressing. Plant tightly and in layers.
4. Many native plant gardens are overwatered and fertilized unnecessarily.
5. Full-sun plants are in part-shade conditions and reaching for light.

A couple of caveats come along with these plans, which you've surely come to anticipate by now. First, nothing—absolutely nothing—can take the place of your site analysis and research on each recommended plant species, especially for your ecoregion. I often share images of a garden space online and have folks ask for a plant list, but a plant list is only one piece of the puzzle. You have to know the plants—and you at least have to read several sources about those plants before you can start placing them in a garden. Even the same plant in a slightly different context will perform differently—a little more competition, a

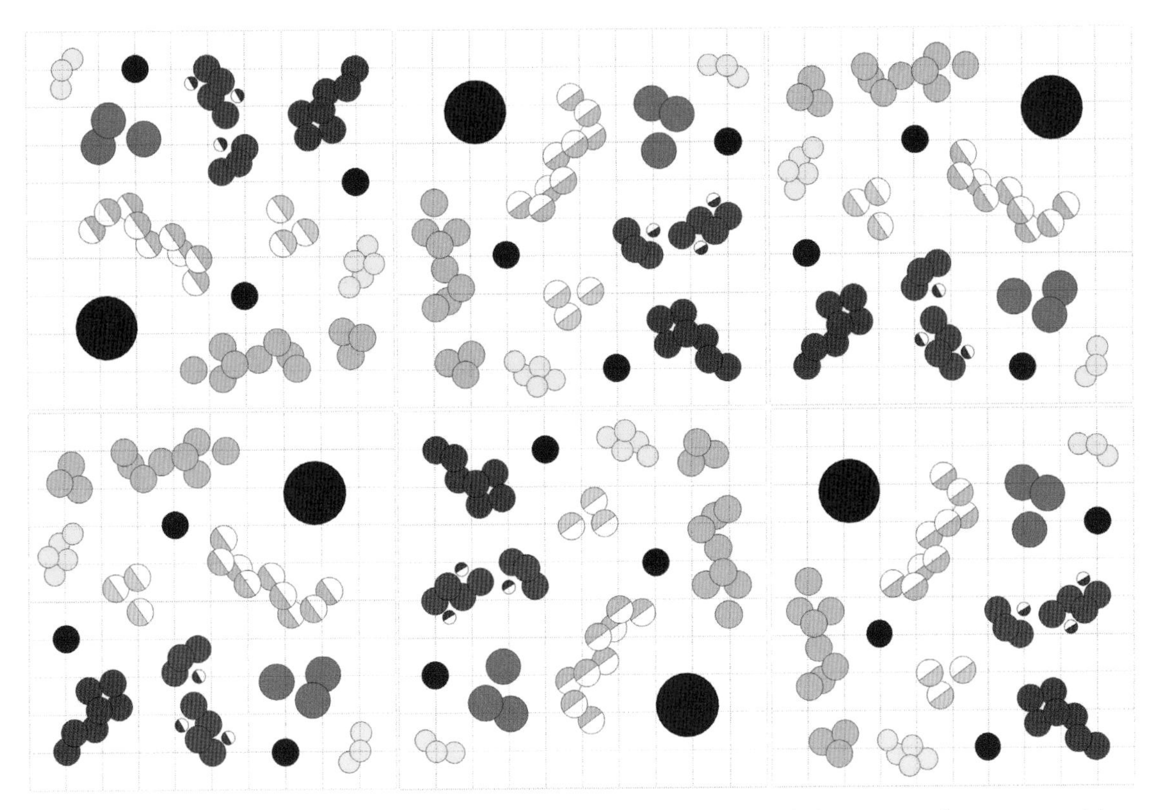

Here is the full-sun garden module laid out for a 600-foot garden. With this approach, you can add plants to fill in gaps and increase massing or drifting to knit together the modules. Your matrix (composed of one or several species) will further tie the garden together.

slight slope, a bit more or less sun—the variables are numerous. And to reiterate what we've been exploring for a while now, the best way to know a plant is to observe it over several years in your garden. You may decide it has to go or you need more, but either way, we have to let the plants teach us, and a plant list is only a best educated guess. Without observation and management, a garden ceases to fulfill its intention. A garden is, after all, a garden—which means you can hardly just plant and forget.

With all that out of the way, let's explore some sample 10x10' modular matrix plans for various site conditions that use perennials, keeping in mind that you may have to make substitutions based on suitability and availability. If you have a larger area, just repeat the module, even turning some of the plans 90 or 180 degrees as you lay out each module's grid. For example, a 1,000' garden will have 10 modules. Now, let's have some fun.

Above: Sideoats grama (*Bouteloua curtipendula*) in bloom. Yes, you will see small bees gathering pollen.

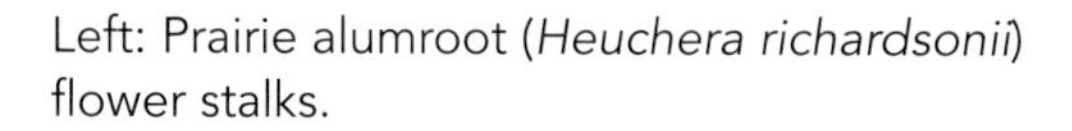

Left: Prairie alumroot (*Heuchera richardsonii*) flower stalks.

Above: Purple poppy mallow (*Callirhoe involucrata*) is an open, intertwining groundcover with a long bloom season.

Left: Rough blazingstar (*Liatris aspera*) in full bud.

GARDEN 1

Full Sun
Dry clay / loamy clay / sandy loam
Matrix: sideoats grama (*Bouteloua curtipendula*), blue grama (*Bouteloua gracilis*), or little bluestem (*Schizachyrium scoparium*)

7 prairie alumroot (*Heuchera richardsonii*)
9 pale purple coneflower (*Echinacea pallida*)
3 slender mountain mint (*Pycnanthemum tenuifolium*)
3 purple poppy mallow (*Callirhoe involucrata*)
7 purple prairie clover (*Dalea purpurea*)
7 black-eyed Susan (*Rudbeckia hirta*)
3 rattlesnake master (*Eryngium yuccifolium*)

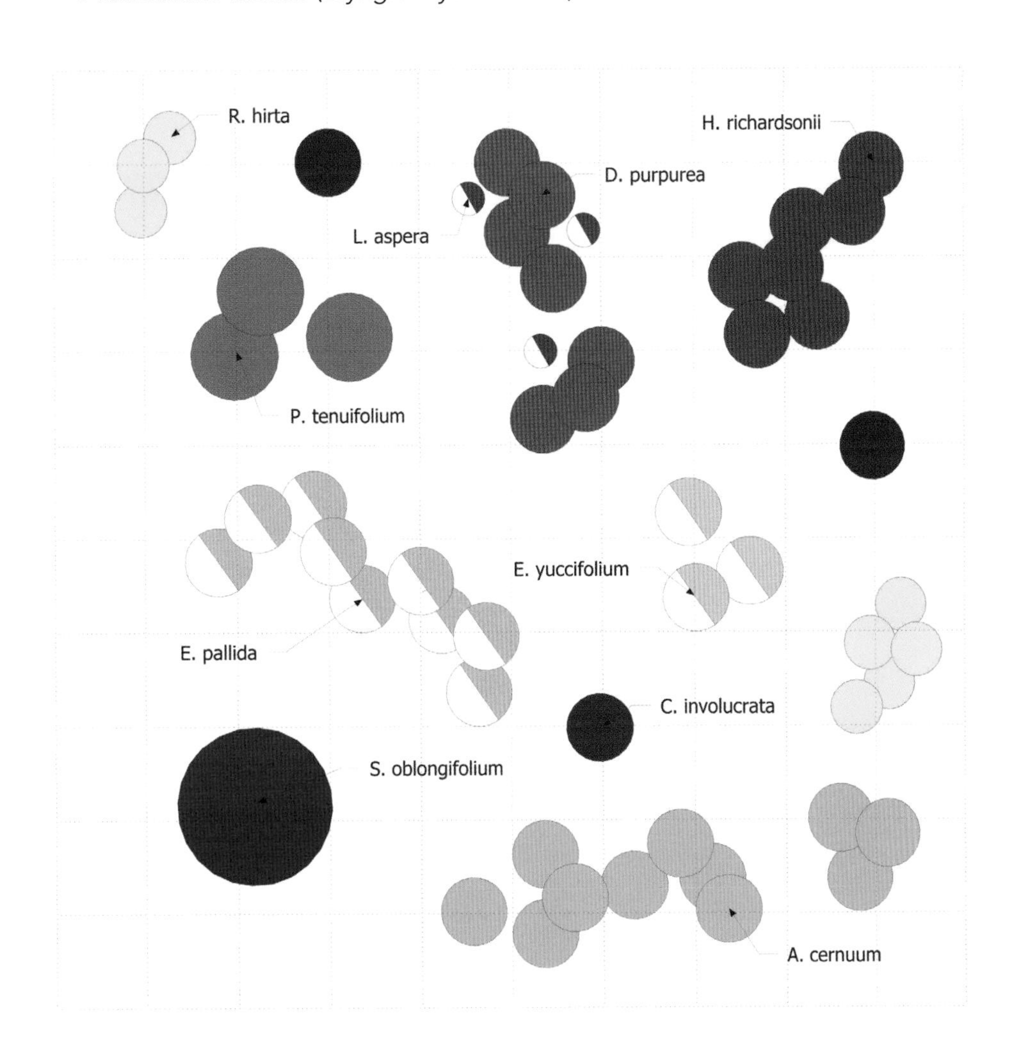

3 rough blazingstar (*Liatris aspera*)
1 aromatic aster (*Symphyotrichum oblongifolium*)
11 nodding onion (*Allium cernuum*)

2 groundcovers
5 seasonal
3 architectural

We're trying to keep these sun-lovers on the shorter side, but in a wet year, they'll all be a little taller. There's a diversity of bloom time, color, and form, as well as some attention paid to root mass and choosing a good number from the aster family.

With this and any of the following designs, there's a lot of wiggle room. For example, not all of these plants may be native to you, but it's likely another within the genus is, or you can sub in something entirely different that fits with the palette and site.

And you certainly don't have to use all these plants or in these quantities. Remember, almost anything is better than a pile of wood mulch. Perhaps you'd prefer a cleaner look while creating an effective ecosystem: removing the *Callirhoe* would be a start, and possibly the *Rudbeckia*, too. Mountain mint will slowly spread in clumps through the grass, competing well, and nodding onion (a bulb) will not fight for the same resources as the grass.

Plant	Habit	Spread	Bloom	Size (w x h)	Known Specialists
Bouteloua curtipendula	G/S	B/M	Su	12 x 18	leonard's skipper, *Hesperia leonardus*
Heuchera richardsonii	G/S	B	Sp	12 x 24	plasterer bee, *Colletes aestivalis*
Echinacea pallida	S/A	B	Su	12 x 30	mining bee, *Andrena helianthiformis*
Pycnanthemum tenuifolium	S	M	Su	24 x 24	hermit sphinx moth, *Lintneria eremitus*
Callirhoe involucrata	G	M	Su	36 x 12	common checkered skipper, *Pyrgus communis*
Dalea purpurea	S	B/M	Su	24 x 18	cellophane bee, *Colletes albescens*
Rudbeckia hirta	S	M	Su	12 x 24	wavy-line emerald moth, *Synchlora aerata*
Eryngium yuccifolium	S	B/M	Su	18 x 40	eryngium borer moth, *Papaipema eryngii*
Allium cernuum	S	B/M	Su	12 x 18	silver noctuid, *Schinia snowi*
Liatris aspera	A	B	Su	12 x 36	glorious flower moth, *Schinia gloriosa*
Symphyotrichum oblongifolium	S	B/M	Fa	36 x 24	long-horned bee, *Melissodes subillatus*

KEY FOR TABLES

Habit:	Spread:	Bloom:
G–groundcover	B–behaved	Sp–spring
S–seasonal bloomer	M–moderate	Su–summer
A–architectural	A–aggressive	Fa–fall

Above: Solomon's seal (*Polygonatum biflorum*) is often used by bumble bee queens gathering pollen to start their new nests.

Left: White-tinged sedge (*Carex albicans*) is highly adaptable but thrives in shady clay soils as a living green mulch.

A female early meadow rue (*Thalictrum dioicum*); males tend to be showier, but both have unique foliage that pairs well with sedge species.

Wild columbine (*Aquilegia canadensis*) is not long-lived but will self-sow in open soils. Expect to see hummingbirds.

GARDEN 2

Full Shade, Dappled Shade, Woodland Edge, Morning Sun
Medium to dry clay / loamy clay / loam
Matrix: white-tinged sedge (*Carex albicans*), curly wood sedge (*Carex rosea*), or sprengel's sedge (*Carex sprengelii*)

3 wild geranium (*Geranium maculatum*)
1 solomon's seal (*Polygonatum biflorum*)
14 wild columbine (*Aquilegia canadensis*)
7 wild phlox (*Phlox divaricata*)
7 early meadow rue (*Thalictrum dioicum*)
7 tall thimbleweed (*Anemone virginiana*)
3 zigzag goldenrod (*Solidago flexicaulis*)
1 calico aster (*Symphyotrichum lateriflorum*) or
3 blue wood aster (*Symphyotrichum cordifolium*)

2 groundcovers
5 seasonal
3 architectural

If you have a site that's dry, even if only in summer, this is the plant list for you. It's well suited for urban locations with a mature tree canopy. *Carex albicans* and *C. rosea* will provide a short, undulating base layer, whereas *Carex sprengelii* has thicker leaves and gets a little taller, but it still has a flowing nature. This garden leans on spring and fall for blooms, but I think that's perfect, because these seasons tend to have a dearth of flowers in home gardens. Let the sunnier areas carry the summer flower load and increase habitat diversity across the landscape.

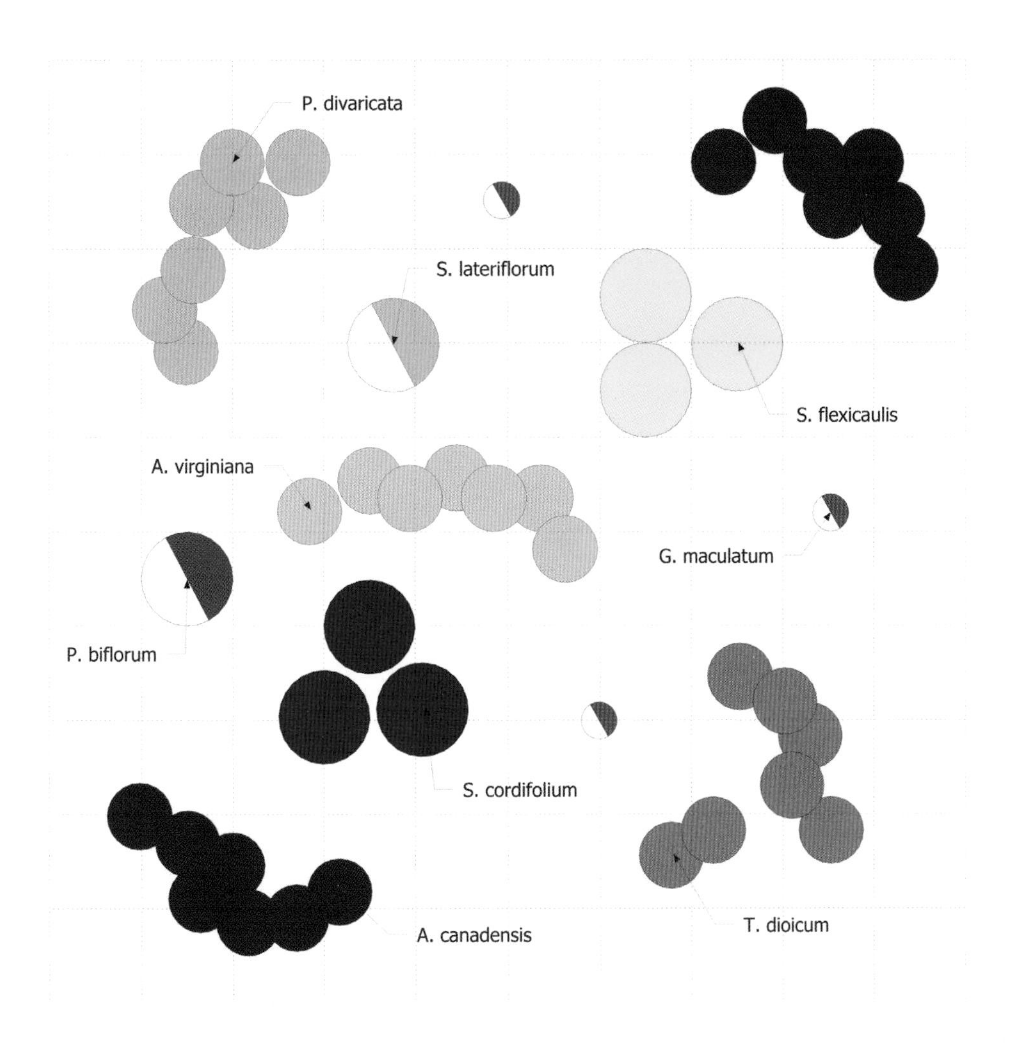

One species might sow aggressively if the cover isn't dense, and that's *Symphyotrichum lateriflorum*. In areas where it can get bright sun in shady areas, or an hour or two of direct light, I find it forms almost an airy hedge about 2–3' tall. But it does put out a lot of seed. It also is absolutely awash in pollinators. You may find an aster that performs better for your site, like blue wood aster. I also want to touch on *Solidago flexicaulis*, which spreads faster by roots in a loose soil than clay; when in bloom, the flowers smell exactly like my grandmother's perfume from the 1980s. Finally, for a little summer color, try tossing in some yellow pimpernel (*Taenidia integerrima*), which provides architectural interest and is host to black swallowtail butterflies.

Plant	Habit	Spread	Bloom	Size (w x h)	Known Specialists
Carex albicans	G/S	B/M	Sp	12 x 12	eyed brown, *Satyrodes eurydice*
Geranium maculatum	G	M	Sp	18 x 12	mining bee, *Andrena distans*
Aquilegia canadensis	S	B/M	Sp	12 x 18	columbine duskywing, *Erynnis lucilius*
Polygonatum biflorum	S	M	Sp	24 x 24	black-patched clepsis moth, *Clepsis melaleucana*
Phlox divaricata	S	B/M	Sp	12 x 12	olive arches moth, *Lacinipolia olivacea*
Thalictrum dioicum	S	B	Sp	18 x 24	Canadian owlet moth, *Calyptra canadensis*
Anemone virginiana	S	B	Su	12 x 24	—
Solidago flexicaulis	S	M	Fa	24 x 24	simple miner bee, *Andrena simplex*
Symphyotrichum lateriflorum	S	M	Fa	24 x 24	pearl crescent, *Phyciodes tharos*

Opposite page: Top left: White wild indigo (*Baptisia alba*) has an open, sculptural form that pairs well with shorter prairie grasses and sedge. Top right: Boneset (*Eupatorium perfoliatum*) was once used as a folk remedy tea purported to treat dengue / breakbone fever. Nearly 200 insect species have been catalogued using boneset. Bottom left: Rattlesnake master (*Erynium yuccifolium*) rises architecturally from other nearby plants, is avoided by herbivores, and has a long season of flower head interest. Bottom right: Zigzag goldenrod (*Solidago flexicaulis*) thrives in dry shade or medium to moist sunny locations. Its fragrance reminds the author of his grandmother's perfume.

GARDEN 3

Half to Full Sun
Moist (not wet) / moderately drained clay / clay loam
Matrix: palm sedge (*Carex muskingumensis*), sprengel's sedge (*Carex sprengelii*), switchgrass (*Panicum virgatum*)

3 Virginia mountain mint (*Pycnanthemum virginianum*)
3 boneset (*Eupatorium perfoliatum*)
5 prairie blazingstar (*Liatris pycnostachya*)
5 blue mistflower (*Conoclinium coelestinum*)
1 white false indigo (*Baptisia alba*)

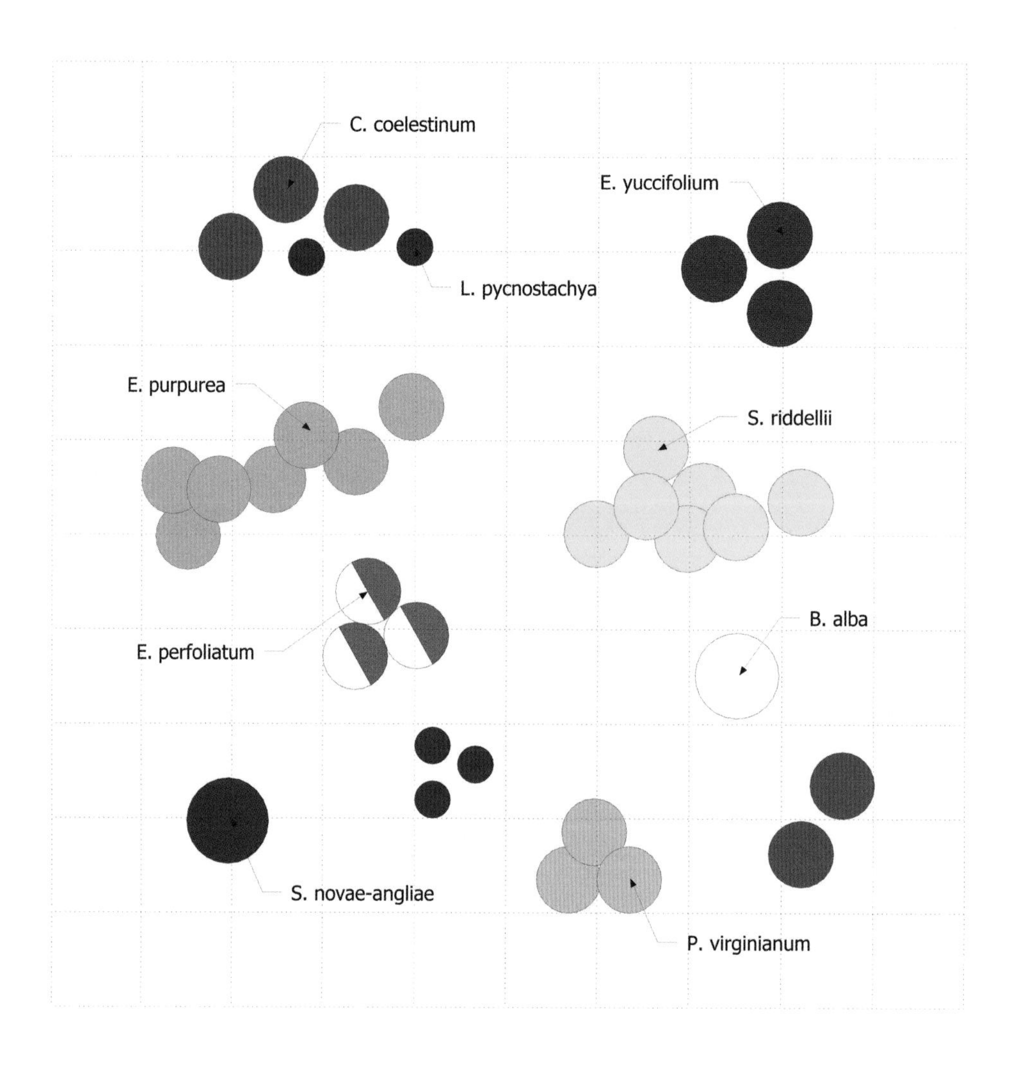

7 purple coneflower (*Echinacea purpurea*)
3 rattlesnake master (*Eryngium yuccifolium*)
7 riddell's goldenrod (*Solidago riddellii*) or zigzag goldenrod (*Solidago flexicaulis*)
1 purple dome aster (*Symphyotrichum novae-angliae* 'Purple Dome')

1 groundcover
5 seasonal
4 architectural

These plants are fairly adaptable, so even if your moist areas tend to dry out for a few weeks—say in high summer—you're good to go. You just don't want mucky soil or standing water, especially not in clay.

Most moisture-loving plants will get taller in a home garden, especially when they are given what they prefer (consistent moisture), so we need to think a little about how they can buttress one another, either through stature (aster) or strong stems (*Echinacea*).

The sedge suggestions are just that, suggestions. I've chosen lower species that will work more as a groundcover matrix. *C. sprengelii* is more a part-shade to shade sedge, which works if it has taller plants around it and / or is in full sun

Plant	Habit	Spread	Bloom	Size (w x h)	Known Specialists
Baptisia alba	A	B	Sp	24 x 48	wild indigo duskywing, *Erynnis baptisiae*
Carex muskingumensis	G	M	Su	24 x 24	tufted sedge moth, *Hypocoena inquinata*
Pycnanthemum virginianum	S	M	Su	24 x 24	purplish-brown looper, *Eutrapela clemataria*
Eupatorium perfoliatum	S	B/M	Su	18 x 36	clymene moth, *Haploa clymene*
Liatris pycnostachya	A	B	Su	12 x 48	bleeding flower moth, *Schinia sanguinea*
Echinacea purpurea	S/A	B/M	Su	12 x 30	silvery checkerspot, *Chlosyne nycteis*
Eryngium yuccifolium	A	B/M	Su	18 x 40	eryngium borer moth, *Papaipema eryngii*
Conoclinium coelestinum	G/S	M	Su/Fa	24 x 18	lined ruby tiger moth, *Phragmatobia lineata*
Solidago flexicaulis	S	M	Fa	24 x 24	brown-hooded owlet, *Cucullia convexipennis*
S. n-a 'Purple Dome'	S	M	Fa	24 x 24	gorgone checkerspot, *Chlosyne gorgone*

Lead plant (*Amorpha canescens*) is a semi-woody perennial best not cut back in spring. Its extensive root system is credited with the zipper sound pioneers heard when plowing up virgin prairie.

Prairie dropseed (*Sporobolus heterolepis*) has a low, flowing form with late-summer flower heads that smell like popcorn or licorice, depending on the person.

but has consistent moisture. *C. muskingumensis* spreads a bit more easily by runners and gets taller—its texture is palm-like and quite different from most sedge; however, its native range is limited to the Midwest. Another option for a matrix cover is prairie dropseed if the soil is well drained, such as a clay loam or sandy loam. Switchgrass will also work, especially with taller forbs, and many selections are available to choose from.

Did you notice the aster cultivar? It's a wild selection—a shorter, less floppy version of the taller, straight species. And there are two goldenrod choices: riddell's may prefer clay soils that are on the moist side, and zigzag—while usually a shadier plant—will do fine in more sun with more moisture. Riddell's goldenrod also has a more limited native range to the upper Midwest.

Showy goldenrod (*Solidago speciosa*) is a critical pollen / nectar source for migrating and overwintering insects. Like all goldenrod species, it does not cause hay fever, since the pollen is heavy and sticky; instead, our native ragweeds with wind-borne pollen are the culprits.

Aromatic aster (*Symphyotrichum oblongifolium*) is a mounding herbaceous perennial that is extremely drought tolerant and often blooms past several freezes.

GARDEN 4

Half to Full Sun, Slope
Clay / clay-loam / sandy loam
Matrix: little bluestem (*Schizachyrium scoparium*), sideoats grama (*Bouteloua curtipendula*), bicknell's sedge (*Carex bicknellii*), or prairie dropseed (*Sporobolus heterolepis*)

10 pale purple coneflower (*Echinacea pallida*)
5 Mexican hat coneflower (*Ratibida columnifera*)
6 slender mountain mint (*Pycnanthemum tenuifolium*)
7 prairie coreopsis (*Coreopsis palmata*)

3 showy goldenrod (*Solidago speciosa*)
1 aromatic aster (*Symphyotrichum oblongifolium*)
7 dotted blazingstar (*Liatris punctata*)
9 black-eyed Susan (*Rudbeckia hirta*)
3 leadplant (*Amorpha canescens*)

1 groundcover
7 seasonal
2 architectural

We're using an assortment of root structures here to keep soil in place at multiple levels, from taproots to corms to fibrous. The focus, though, is on fibrous-rooted plants like grasses and sedge. Of course, any time you have an

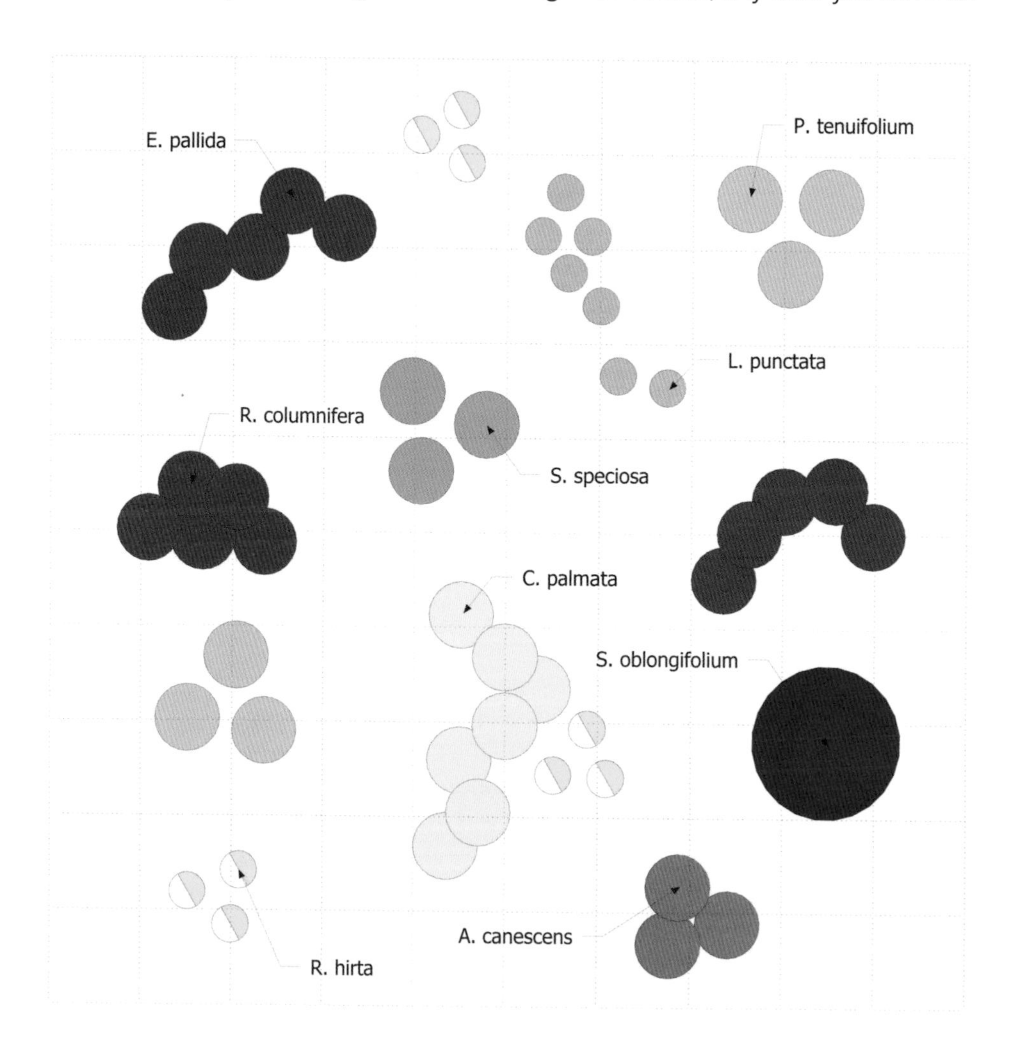

erosion-prone site, not only are roots important, but so, too, is dense vegetation, which can break and hold rainfall.

We also need to think about reproduction habit. *Coreopsis* and *Pycnanthemum* will spread readily by roots, mingling among the grass and sedge. We'll see a little self-sowing from the *Ratibida* and *Solidago*. And the *Amorpha* and *Symphyotrichum* are shrub-like in their form, which will cover more ground and provide more surface area in their branches to hold water (plus the former has a thick root zone and the latter will run by root a little). All plants are fairly drought tolerant once established.

If you are planting on a slope and want to get that matrix going ASAP, you have a few choices: 1) if it's mid-spring or early summer, get your flower plugs in and then sow in warm-season bunch grasses, keep moist until germination; 2) if it's fall, plug sedge or grasses on 8–12" centers. The sooner you can plug warm-season grasses, the better to get enough rooting before freezes. You could also plug the matrix in spring. In all cases, and if it's a steep slope or highly erosion prone, a straw blanket may be a good investment and should be installed after seeding but before planting (you can plant plugs in the netting by spreading it apart).

Plant	Habit	Spread	Bloom	Size (w x h)	Known Specialists
Bouteloua curtipendula	S/G	B/M	Su	18 x 24	dakota skipper, *Hesperia dacotae*
Echinacea pallida	S/A	B/M	Su	12 x 30	silvery checkerspot, *Chlosyne nycteis*
Ratibida columnifera	S	B/M	Su	12 x 24	wavy-lined emerald, *Synchlora aerata*
Pycnanthemum tenuifolium	S	M	Su	24 x 24	hermit sphinx moth, *Lintneria eremitus*
Coreopsis palmata	S	M	Su	18 x 24	tickseed long-horned bee, *Melissodes coreopsis*
Rudbeckia hirta	S/A	M	Su	12 x 24	coneflower miner, *Andrena rudbeckiae*
Amorpha canescens	S/A	B	Su	24 x 24	southern dogface, *Zerene cesonia*
Liatris punctata	S	B	Su	18 x 18	bleeding flower moth, *Schinia sanguinea*
Solidago speciosa	S	M	Fa	18 x 36	goldenrod cellophane bee, *Melissodes solidaginis*
Symphyotrichum oblongifolium	S	M	Fa	36 x 24	silvery checkerspot, *Chlosyne nycteis*

A Note on Combining the New with the Old

If you have an established bed, it's simple enough to use these plans with what you already have. It's likely that you will first be removing what you don't want, after which it's literally a matter of sliding in or superimposing the grid, then tweaking placement to make sure the plant communities are in the right places for aesthetics and ecosystem function.

However, if your current bed is very thick and you won't be removing much—just plugging gaps—there's another strategy to take. By this point, you've so thoroughly researched the plants that you know their below- and above-ground habit, so you can match those parameters to the habit of the current plants in your beds. So let's say you leave all those heirloom daylilies, knowing they stay mostly in one clump and then the foliage gets ugly about midsummer, needing to be covered up. Planting something that grows 2' tall and can finger through the daylilies seems like a good idea, and you can start with a matrix of sedge or short bunchgrasses. From that point, you could add masses of pollinator-supporting *Pycnanthemum tenuifolium and Symphyotrichum oblongifolium*, and employ a weaving groundcover (*Callirhoe involucrata*). Maybe adding some sculptural plants is in the cards—*Baptisia alba* or *B. minor*, *Liatris aspera*, and *Solidago speciosa*. I think any stand of daylily or hosta would look more pleasing—and be more resilient and accommodating to wildlife—if it became a mass within a grassy / sedgy matrix. In fact, I suspect almost every mature garden bed could successfully take a green-mulch plugging of sedge or bunchgrasses beneath established perennials and woodies.

Remember, your goal is to cover the ground in layers to add diversity of structure, bloom type, and bloom time. Using the above modules, even piecemeal, can help you integrate ecological complexity, function, and resilience within any existing plantscape.

Final Thought

At the beginning of this book is a quote by famed landscape architect Jens Jensen, who was a Danish immigrant and part of the prairie school movement along with Frank Lloyd Wright. Jensen designed public and private gardens across the Midwest, primarily in Illinois, Iowa, and Wisconsin, as well as extensive landscapes for the Ford family in Michigan. He focused on using native plants and bringing a bit of the expansive prairie into our built environment. When Jensen called for "no clipped hedges," he meant plants should be allowed to find their way, that we should see beauty in their natural forms and celebrate

Formal frames can help make a wilder bed appear more intentional and accepting. © Nick McCullough. Used with permission.

Native plants can even be used on their own in formal design, as this garden at the Mt. Cuba Center illustrates.

their inherent wildness. For us, though, perhaps we should reconsider clipped hedges if they can smartly inscribe or outline a wildness brought home. A meadow bed juxtaposed with a clipped hedge, even if an exotic boxwood, might be just the thing we need to bridge the gap between a garden that some would call weedy and others would call liberating and life-giving. It's time to rethink pretty. Prairie up.

In late autumn the dynamic structure of this front yard garden becomes more evident, showing off a combination of strategies behind the design. Employed here are cues to care, bloom and leaf color succession, winter interest, a diversity of plant layers, as well as negative space in the form of a lawn hellstrip, which helps tie the space into the larger neighborhood.

5

RESOURCES

The annotations in this chapter are meant to both round out your work as a garden manager and help you implement the design of your prairie-inspired garden space. For example, learning about the history of grasslands alongside which plants are host for which species, coupled with the ability to identify seedlings, will go a long way in strengthening your gardening skills. While you may not want to explore all these sources right now, as you develop and grow, they may come in handy. Particularly useful are the appendices and bibliographies at the end of each book mentioned, while the websites will surely take you down a good rabbit hole.

I've found all these sources personally and professionally useful, and while there are many more I could add, this list presents a well-rounded starting point for gardeners at almost any level. Keep in mind there are infinitely more regional sources, from plant guidebooks to gardening in your climate, that mirror the following material.

Finding Native Plants

The Xerces Society

This is one of the primary starter sources for building out a plant list arranged by region. Since Xerces is an organization that advocates for science-based invertebrate conservation, you'll also find a wealth of information via its many publications on best practices, wildland restoration, gardening, and more.

Pollinator Partnership

Offering a plethora of national programs on pollinator monitoring, Pollinator Partnership is the founder of Pollinator Week, which happens every June. On its website, you'll find regional guides that provide background on your ecoregion, plant lists, host plants for pollinators, and much more.

University Extensions

Many land grant universities have extension services, not to mention arboretums. They often are excellent resources for local and regional topics such as plant choices, management, pests, and weed identification. In my state, we're lucky to have the Nebraska Statewide Arboretum (NSA), which is a network of landscapes for various Plains ecoregions. NSA has a wealth of publications to help native plant and wildlife gardeners across flyover country, so even if you don't live in Nebraska, it's worth checking out.

USDA (U.S. Department of Agriculture)

With the USDA's ecoregion maps and plants database, you can quickly discover whether a plant is native to you based on a county-level map by entering Latin or common names (Latin is always preferred, because common names can refer to multiple species). The plants database also includes a fact sheet and plant guide to help you learn more about each species.

BONAP (Biota of North America Program)

More advanced and detailed than the USDA Plants Database, BONAP provides nuanced information for your geographical region and ecoregion. You can not only search plants to see if they are native but also perform research on local hydrology, climate, and more. All this information will increase your capabilities in plant selection and management through the years, especially as you learn from wild plant communities nearby.

Spring Creek Prairie, a tallgrass remnant of southeastern Nebraska, in its fine winter garb and still hard at work providing habitat for 222 bird and 53 butterfly species.

Plant Native–http://www.plantnative.org/index.htm

This website is a slightly out of date, but nonetheless invaluable, database to find native plant nurseries, landscapers, and organizations in your state. Some of the listings may no longer exist, or they may have moved (virtually or physically), so an internet search of that listing is wise before moving on. This site also includes an introductory, though handy, twelve-step guide to "naturescaping."

A camouflaged looper moth larvae (*Synchlora aerata*) has disguised itself by placing petals of sweet coneflower (*Rudbeckia subtomentosa*) along its body.

Izel Native Plants

This online marketplace works with wholesalers, which usually supply plants only to professionals, and regional native plant nurseries. The biggest advantage is you can order plugs, which are cost effective and establish quickly, in large-quantity trays of 32 and 50. Izel works with regional suppliers from the Midwest to all points east, ensuring you get local plants suited for your area.

Learning about Native Plants

Bplant.org

This site is as close to one-stop shopping as you can get when learning about specific native plants. Simply type in the scientific or common name and get taken to a profile page with links to reliable websites that provide more information. Bplant also features a clickable ecoregion map that takes you from level 1 to level 4 ecoregions, which makes learning about your home ground a bit simpler.

Prairie Moon Nursery

This is one of the go-to sources to learn the basic needs and behaviors of many native plant species. An added bonus is that this nursery provides information on seeds per ounce and germination codes, so if you are seeding or growing plants from seed, you're good to go.

Prairie Nursery and Missouri Botanical Gardens (MOBOT)

I'm lumping these together because they are two more go-to sources for learning about specific native plant species. Prairie Nursery, like Prairie Moon Nursery, also has prep and seeding guides to create your own meadow space that are well worth the read. The Missouri Botanical Garden provides plant profiles and extensive databases of both native and exotic garden plants from around the world.

Illinois Wildflowers–illinoiswildflowers.info

This is perhaps the number-one source of information if you are anywhere near the middle of the country—but even well beyond. Plant profiles share a wealth of information, from characteristics to habitat needs, as well as insect and bug species that use the plant as a host. Further, it provides a database of adult insect species observed using flowers from a plethora of plant species.

Jon Farrar. *Field Guide to Wildflowers of Nebraska and the Great Plains.* 2nd ed. Iowa City: University of Iowa Press, 2011.

Jon Farrar's important guidebook details hundreds of Plains and Midwest species, many of which are also found in the entire eastern half of the country and into the mountain West. Each plant profile provides growth habit, life cycle, and site requirements in an easy-to-find method based on flower color.

Claude Barr. *Jewels of the Plains.* Minneapolis: University of Minnesota Press, 2015.

Barr's book contains seminal observations of High Plains native plants, many of which are native far beyond his western South Dakota, northern Nebraska, and eastern Wyoming homeground. The updated 2015 edition by Jim Locklear provides modern Latin names for accurate researching.

Alan Branhagen. *Native Plants of the Midwest.* Portland: Timber Press, 2016.

This is a fairly comprehensive guide of our most garden-worthy natives and native cultivars, covering everything from woody and evergreen shrubs and trees to herbaceous perennials and annuals for all layers. Each profile briefly discusses the plant's preferred growing conditions, how to use it in a bed, and other attributes. It's a terrific starting point for finding new plants.

Heather Holm. *Pollinators of Native Plants: Attract, Observe, and Identify Pollinators and Beneficial Insects with Native Plants.* Minnetonka: Pollination Press, 2014.

The core benefit of this text are the native plant profiles, which feature some of the more prominent pollinator species that use each plant, alongside the how and why. An introduction to pollination and how plants communicate with pollinators begins the exploration, allowing gardeners to think in new ways about how they select plants for their landscape.

Charlotte Adelman and Bernard Schwartz. *The Midwestern Native Garden: Native Alternatives to Nonnative Flowers and Plants.* Athens: Ohio University Press, 2011.

Categorized by season, commonly used exotic plants in the ornamental trade are presented alongside native plants that appear and / or perform similarly

Prairie-inspired gardens become the next stage in suburban ecosystem succession after lawn.

in the same site. Growing conditions are outlined for each plant, along with a few pollinator species that particularly benefit from the natives mentioned.

Designing and Managing the Garden

Roy Diblik. *The Know Maintenance Perennial Garden.* Portland: Timber Press, 2014.

After taking note of the shortcomings of most traditional landscape methods, Diblik helps gardeners prepare, plan, implement, and manage perennial plant beds through an understanding of how the plants work. With a calming, reassuring, and humble voice, this book takes you through detailed plant lists—both native and non—and finally into a variety of sample plans with useful plant combinations that work over time. Diblik's introduction to resilient landscapes is a wonderful primer based on years of trial and error.

Thomas Rainer and Claudia West. *Planting in a Post-Wild World.* Portland: Timber Press, 2015.

In this deeper dive into the world of plant communities, Rainer and West take time to explore the issues at stake in urban environments and what a new kind of planting means for the health of people and wildlife. This book is probably for the more advanced reader with some experience under their belt, but it is a game-changer in the field of landscape design and landscape architecture by putting plants first.

The Xerces Society. *Gardening for Butterflies.* Portland: Timber Press, 2016.

Much more than a science-based text on how to support and attract butterfly species to your home garden, this book delves into complex issues such as using exotic plants, as well as how to garden for moths. Plant installation, design, and maintenance are touched on, but the real wealth is found in the data on how native plants and specific garden structure can support insects year-round.

Jessica Walliser. *Attracting Beneficial Bugs to Your Garden.* Portland: Timber Press, 2013.

Defining beneficial bugs, complete with profiles of those most commonly found in the garden, Walliser's book delves even deeper by exploring the best plants to support beneficial bugs and how to design a landscape for them. This natural, organic method of creating an ecosystem by inviting species we've been taught to fear will elevate your design for deeper function.

Sue Reed and Ginny Stibolt. *Climate-Wise Landscaping.* Gabriola Island, British Columbia: New Society Publishers, 2018.

With climate change affecting how resilient our gardens can be, it's more important than ever to consider all facets of ecosystem function when designing a landscape. Reed and Stibolt use science-based information to explore such topics as sustainable lawn care, using woody plants to cool structures and sequester carbon, how to use plants to manage stormwater flow, and building soil. A wealth of information exists here to fine-tune and re-imagine all facets of garden design in a time of climate disruption, from site prep and materials used to plant selection and arrangement.

Access to diverse natural structure increases a child's cognitive ability, levels of creativity, and ability to work well with others—not to mention the physical health benefits of coming into contact with myriad microorganisms that can mitigate the development of allergies. Kids don't need lawn to play in.

Learning about Grasslands and Prairies

Paul Johnsgard. *The Ecology of a Tallgrass Treasure.* Lincoln: Zea Books, 2018.

While this text focuses on one tallgrass remnant in eastern Nebraska, it is far more representative than 800 acres. Johnsgard not only catalogs species at Spring Creek Prairie but also provides countless details about those species whose ranges extend across the Plains and Midwest. These partial lists are illustrative of the forb, graminoid, and faunal diversity we should expect to see within intact remnants and even some restored areas.

Candace Savage. *Prairie: A Natural History.* Vancouver: Greystone Books, 2011.

A plethora of books explore the rich, complex history of North American grasslands (including the natural and social history), but this book has always been a mainstay. Savage takes us patiently through the geologic and geographic history, using science along the way to discuss water, soil, plants, and the conversion of grasslands to human use. This book is simply overflowing with information that will ground any native plant gardener in their wild community.

Annick Smith. ***Big Bluestem: Journey into the Tallgrass.*** **Tulsa: Council Oak Books, 1996.**

If you want to dig deeper into one region of the central United States, perhaps using it as an analog for others, Smith's personal and historical narrative of the Tallgrass Prairie Preserve of northeast Oklahoma is a good place to start. Combined with evocative photographs, this book weaves geographic and biologic history with the culture of the Osage tribe alongside the pressure of oil booms and homesteading.

Chris Helzer. ***The Ecology and Management of Prairies in the Central United States.*** **Iowa City: University of Iowa Press, 2010.**

This book is a slightly more technical though superbly readable guide on managing a prairie restoration. It contains plenty of nuggets that can be translated to managing a garden space, including such topics as setting objectives, working with drought, and cultivating biodiversity. One of this book's benefits is learning how various methods of disturbance (such as fire and mowing) can increase or decrease various plant species and affect wildlife, depending on when and how they are applied.

Plant Identification

Dave Williams. ***The Prairie In Seed.*** **Iowa City: University of Iowa Press, 2016.**

Guidebooks on grass and wildflower identification are plenty, but there's little on accurately naming plants when they've gone to seed. Organized by seed head type, you'll learn basic concepts to make more complex plant identification possible in fall and winter—as well as gain an appreciation for the beauty of native prairie plants long after their blooms fade away. Each plant description covers habitat type as well as how to gather and clean the seed. As with other books mentioned in this chapter, the plants covered tend to have very wide ranges in the continental United States and are not limited to the Great Plains and Midwest.

Dave Williams. ***The Tallgrass Prairie Guide to Seed and Seedling Identification in the Upper Midwest.*** **Iowa City: University of Iowa Press, 2010.**

A handy guide for some of the most common prairie plants in the wild, this book is essential for home gardeners. It helps identify native species that are fill-

Mason bee mothers hard at work in early summer provisioning and sealing off their nest. Like most native bee species, they are reticent to sting; some species have females with no stinger, and males have none at all.

ing in so that, while weeding, you don't pull a desired seedling as your garden develops naturally. Each profile provides information on site conditions, comparison to similar species, and seed germination requirements.

James Stubbendieck, Mitchell Coffin, and L. M. Landholt. *Weeds of the Great Plains.* Lincoln: Nebraska Department of Agriculture, 2003.

While becoming harder to get your hands on, this 600-page behemoth is filled with information on a wide variety of common weeds in both rural and urban areas. The benefit for home gardeners is being able to not only identify a weed but also learn about its life cycle, potential benefits and drawbacks, and how to manage it. You'll get all of this and more for both native and exotic plant species (admittedly, some of which wildlife gardeners would be hard-pressed to call weeds). This book is handy specifically because it can help us realize how much or how little we need to manage a particular weed species.

Citizen Science and Wildlife Observation

USA National Phenology Network–usanpn.org

This network reports and tracks both plant and animal life stages, such as when a tree blooms and when a bird species starts nesting. Quantifying these events helps us understand how climate change is affecting landscapes and how species may or may not be adapting. Phenological information can be especially important when it comes to fauna and flora with co-evolved mutualisms or co-dependencies, such as bees and flowers.

Jarrod Fowler–jarrodfowler.com

Online publications by this expert in native bees highlights pollen specialist bees of the western, central, and eastern United States. Fowler also provides lists of specific plant families, genera, and species that support the roughly 30 percent of bees that are pollen specialists. These lists are essential in learning how to make the best plant selections and habitat design to support pollinators.

Joseph S. Wilson and Olivia Messinger Carril. *The Bees in Your Backyard*. Princeton: Princeton University Press, 2015.

Some 900 full-color images help you identify the bees visiting your landscape and document the plants that they tend to use, as well as why they use them. With such detailed information based on your observations at home, you'll be better able to fine-tune garden beds for maximum bee support.

iNaturalist–inaturalist.org

iNat is an app that helps you track and identify wildlife in your garden and on excursions in the wild. Ultimately, it's an online social network for both serious and weekend ecologists that builds a set of biodiversity data to track ecosystem health in various habitats. Some of the most important discoveries of threatened species or those believed to be extirpated from an area come from citizen scientists on this site.

BugGuide–bugguide.net

Similar to iNaturalist but focused on invertebrates (insects, bugs, spiders), anyone can submit photos for identification by experts, as well as use the platform to make identifications on their own. This site is an incredibly useful tool for understanding who is using your landscape and how to support them via further research.

A black swallowtail nectars on purple coneflower.

A CANDID Q&A

Is butterfly bush helpful to pollinators?

If we're referring to *Buddleia davidii* and its cultivars, no, it isn't helpful. First, butterfly bush is not a larval host plant for any insect species in North America. Second, the nectar is only accessible to long-tongued adults, which is why you'll see primarily butterflies, bumble bees, and hummingbird moths using it. Finally, butterfly bush is spreading aggressively in several parts of the country, from the Pacific Northwest to Appalachia, and now some Midwestern grasslands as birds disperse the seed far and wide. In other words, it's showing the potential to be invasive by creating a monoculture and limiting biodiversity. Is your cultivar "seedless"? There's nothing a plant wants more than to reproduce, so nature will find a way. Butterfly bush has benefited from a marketable common name that doesn't adequately represent its many shortcomings. There are a plethora of better options.

Shouldn't people just accept my wilder garden as it is? I find it beautiful, and I see so many species using it throughout the year.

That would be nice, but if we're going to win hearts and minds, it might be best to meet people somewhere near the middle—and doing so won't lessen the beauty for you or wildlife. So work on removing native species that spread too aggressively or get too tall, and reconsider how to create more massing and tiers alongside cues to care. Keeping plants short or in somewhat legible

arrangements doesn't drastically reduce ecosystem function—it may be easier for pollinators to find a group of three asters when flying overhead. And no matter what, your landscape is still leaps and bounds healthier than a managed lawn or mulch-dominated bed.

Hosta and astilbe are the only flowering plants I've found that grow well in full shade—there just don't seem to be many herbaceous perennial options that are native.

Here's a partial list that doesn't even include many ephemerals:

Calico aster (*Symphyotrichum lateriflorum*)
Blue wood aster (*Symphyotrichum cordifolium*)
Short's aster (*Symphyotrichum shortii*)
Big leaf aster (*Eurybia macrophylla*)
Wild geranium (*Geranium maculatum*)
Wild columbine (*Aquilegia canadensis*)
Zigzag goldenrod (*Solidago flexicaulis*)
Blue-stemmed goldenrod (*Solidago caesia*)
Solomon's seal (*Polygonatum biflorum*)
Early meadow rue (*Thalictrum dioicum*)
Hairy wood mint (*Blephilia hirsuta*)
Black cohosh (*Cimicifuga racemosa*)
Wild golden glow (*Rudbeckia laciniata*)
Dutchman's breeches (*Dicentra cucullaria*)
Solomon's plume (*Maianthemum racemosum*)
Virginia bluebells (*Mertensia virginica*)
Wild blue phlox (*Phlox divaricata*)
Jacob's ladder (*Polemonium reptans*)
Golden groundsel (*Packera aurea*)
White snakeroot (*Ageratina altissima*)

Are there any grassy options for shade?

White-tinged sedge (*Carex albicans*)
Curly wood sedge (*Carex rosea*)
Eastern star sedge (*Carex radiata*)
Ivory sedge (*Carex eburnea*)
Common wood sedge (*Carex blanda*)
Sprengel's sedge (*Carex sprengelii*)
Penn sedge (*Carex pensylvanica*)
Texas sedge (*Carex texensis*)
Common bur sedge (*Carex grayi*)
Bottlebrush grass (*Elymus hystrix*)

I should be yanking all my thistles because they're noxious weeds, right?

There certainly are some invasive thistles that will be listed as noxious weeds in your county, including musk, bull, and Canada thistle. However, a plethora of native thistles are highly beneficial to adult pollinators, including pasture thistle (*Cirsium discolor*) and tall thistle (*C. altissimum*). These species tend to be much more behaved, especially in a dense plant community they evolved alongside, and many bloom in the critical shoulder season of late summer into early fall. Native thistles are almost always identifiable by their silvery underleaf.

I have seasonal allergies, so what I can plant instead of goldenrod for fall blooms?

Goldenrod (*Solidago* spp., *Oligoneuron* spp.) have sticky, heavy pollen that is not airborne; goldenrod is insect pollinated. However, our native ragweeds (*Ambrosia artemisiifolia* and *A. trifida*) can look similar to a few goldenrod species. Ragweed is wind pollinated—which means ragweed is the likely culprit. Along with asters, goldenrods are a powerhouse of food for adult pollinators.

Won't a nature-based garden attract pests like snakes, mice, spiders, and ticks?

Yes. A nature-based garden means you are inviting nature into your life. But it's important to learn about the fauna using your space so you can live more aware. If you reside in an area with venomous snakes, take time to learn about those species and where they prefer to hang out and areas they avoid; you may find that you don't want to have a rock pile or that you should create large sitting areas of gravel and mulch. Remember, snakes eat mice. Spiders are crucial, beneficial predators that prey on true pests in our landscapes, so again, identify and research the species you see to assuage your fears. As for ticks, author David Quammen in *Spillover* shows how fragmented habitats increase deer ticks that carry Lyme disease because of a vicious cycle: fragmentation leads to fewer predators (foxes, owls) which leads to an increase of white-footed mice, which leads to an increase of ticks carrying lyme disease. If you have a wilder garden, widen the pathway to 6 feet, since ticks love to hang out on the tips of arching stems, where they attempt to hitchhike, and be sure to wear repellent, tuck pants into socks, and check yourself thoroughly. Contact with nature is just too important for our mental and physical health; we must strive to create designed ecosystems that rebuild natural processes, which, in turn, create more predator / prey balance.

How can I help struggling honey bee populations, since they are critical pollinators?

Collectively, when it comes to effective pollination, our 3,500+ species of native bees are far superior to European honey bees, the latter of which are used in agricultural farming of monocultures. In some ways, "saving the honey bee" to help bees is like saving turkeys to help threatened grassland birds. Wild honey bee populations are globally stable. Unfortunately, honey bees create added pressure on native bee populations through their high numbers, large forage range, and ability to spread disease when visiting blooms. As we lose large areas of prairie and hedgerows in rural and suburban areas, native bees and other beneficial insects and bugs vanish that could otherwise pollinate and control pests for free.

Recent research shows insects like syrphid flies are pollinators that can be superior to honey bees, increasing strawberry yields alone by 70 percent. While considered generalists, they have the ability to learn which flower color provides the best nectar on specific plants, making them temporary specialists (many bee species share this trait). Syrphids fill a pollinator niche that larger bee species may not. They also increase ecosystem services through their larvae, which are voracious predators of aphids, thrips, leafhoppers, mealybugs, and whiteflies.

And let's not discount the pollination value of our 11,000 moth species. There's so much we continue to learn about our world and how fauna interact with flora.

Are bee and butterfly houses helpful?

Butterfly houses are never used by butterflies—although they may make nice homes for beneficial predators like some wasp species. Bee houses tend to support just 25 percent of our native bees that are cavity-nesting (the other 75 percent live in bare soil, so to support them, don't mulch too thickly or at all), and disease issues can creep in with bee house use. For example, if you are using hollowed tubes (wood or fiber), these need to be disposed of after adults leave during the subsequent year, as reuse could spread disease. Drilled nesting blocks should not be reused. Bee houses may also be magnets for predators like woodpeckers—in the wild, nesting sites are more scattered and hidden, which may increase survival rates. In general, the smaller the bee house, the better to reduce predation and disease transmission.

When should I clean up the garden?

Definitely not in fall. Leave it standing to provide food and shelter for bees, butterflies, frogs, birds, and so much more. In early spring, cut perennial stems back to about 12–18", as leaving this length provides ideal homes for native, cavity-nesting bees. I find the most used plant stems are *Coreopsis tripteris, Agastache foeniculum, Echinacea purpurea, Monarda fistulosa*, and some *Symphyotrichum* and *Asclepias* species. Anything you cut down can be immediately placed on the ground as free mulch / fertilizer and more habitat.

What are your essential tools?

A serrated soil knife, small garden spade with a D handle, bypass pruner, switchblade, fire hose nozzle, expandable garden hose (not the coiled kind), and knee pads are all my essentials. For looser soil—clay loam, loam, loess—I use a good cordless (18 volt +) or corded drill (7 amps +) with a 3" wide soil auger bit. I've found corded mixing drills, which have lower rpm and higher torque designed to handle mortar and adhesive mud, do not burn out in heavier soil like standard drills and are the best option for doing hundreds of plugs. Make sure to use a 10–12 gauge power cord (important for longer runs) and a solid steel auger bit, like those made by the Garden Auger at gardenauger.com. At the top of the power tool spectrum would be a cordless mixing drill; with a backup battery or two and a good auger bit, this setup could run you $500-$600.

What's your number-one piece of advice for designing a prairie garden that's pleasing to both humans and wildlife?

Start small, not necessarily in garden or plant size but in plant species. Whether you have 2,000 or 200 square feet to work with, consider selecting just 10 forb species to begin with, and place them in sizable mingling groups and drifts through a grass or sedge matrix. Over the first few years, you can observe their growth and the site conditions, learn how to tweak and manage the layered garden using a matrix design, and then slowly add plants that fill in and diversify various niches (groundcover, seasonal flowers, architectural, host plants, erosion control). Let the plants show you where to go. Celebrate change as an opportunity to excel.

BIBLIOGRAPHY

Albertson, F. W., and J. E. Weaver. "Nature and Degree of Recovery of Grassland from the Great Drought of 1933–1940." In *Ecological Monographs*. Ecological Society of America, 1944.

Angelella, G. M. et al. "Honey Bee Hives Decrease Wild Bee Abundance, Species Richness, and Fruit Count on Farms Regardless of Wildflower Strips." *Scientific Reports* (February 5, 2021).

Beck, Travis. *Principles of Ecological Design*. Washington: Island Press, 2013.

Doyle, Toby et al. "Pollination by Hoverflies in the Anthropocene." *Proceedings of the Royal Society B* (May 20, 2020).

Fargione, Joseph E. at al. "Natural Climate Solutions for the United States." *Science Advances* (November 14, 2018).

Fitch, Gordon et al. "Changes in Adult Sex Ratio in Wild Bee Communities Are Linked to Urbanization." *Nature Scientific Reports* (March 6, 2019).

Forister, Matthew L., Emma M. Pelton, and Scott H. Black, "Declines in Insect Abundance and Diversity: We Know Enough to Act Now." *Conservation Science and Practice* (June 22, 2019).

Gilman, Jeff. *The Truth about Organic Gardening: Benefits, Drawbacks, and the Bottom Line*. Portland Timber Press, 2008.
Hamblin, April L. et al. "Wild Bee Abundance Declines with Urban Warming, Regardless of Floral Density." *Urban Ecosystems* (January 31, 2018).
Hanski, Ilkka et al. "Environmental Biodiversity, Human Microbiota, and Allergy are Interrelated." *Proceedings of the National Academy of Sciences of the United States of America* (May 22, 2012).
Hung, Keng-Lou James et al. "Non-Native Honey Bees Disproportionately Dominate the Most Abundant Floral Resources in a Biodiversity Hotspot." *Proceedings of the Royal Society B* (February 20, 2019).
Kennen, Kate and Niall Kirkwood. *Phyto: Principles and Resources for Site Remediation and Landscape Design*. New York Routledge, 2015.
Koski, Matthew H. et al. "Floral Pigmentation Has Responded Rapidly to Global Change in Ozone and Temperature." *Current Biology* (September 17, 2020).
Mateos, David Moreno et al. "Anthropogenic Ecosystem Disturbance and the Recovery Debt." *Nature Communications* (January 20, 2017).
Mateos, David Moreno. "How Ecosystems Recover from Ancient Human Impacts." Lecture, Department of Landscape Architecture, Graduate School of Design, Harvard (April 21, 2020).
Nassauer, Joan I. "Messy Ecosystems, Orderly Frames." *Landscape Journal* (Fall 1995).
Owens, Avalon C. S. et al. "Light Pollution Is a Driver of Insect Declines." *Biological Conservation* (September 20, 2019).
Rainer, Thomas and Claudia West. *Planting in a Post-Wild World.* Portland: Timber Press, 2015.
Roberts, Caleb et al. "Shifting Avian Spatial Regimes in a Changing Climate." *Nature Climate Change* (June 24, 2019).
Sales, Kris et al. "Experimental Heatwaves Compromise Sperm Function and Cause Transgenerational Damage in a Model Insect." *Nature Communications* (November 3, 2018).
Savage, Candace. *Prairie: A Natural History*. Vancouver: Greystone Books, 2011.
Smith, Adam et al. "Phenotypic Distribution Models Corroborate Species Distribution Models: A Shift in the Role and Prevalence of a Dominant Prairie Grass in Response to Climate Change." *Global Change Biology* (February 17, 2017).
Walton, Richard E. et al. "Nocturnal Pollinators Strongly Contribute to Pollen Transport of Wild Flowers in an Agricultural Landscape." *Biology Letters* (May 13, 2020).
Warren, Rachel et al. "The Projected Effect on Insects, Vertebrates, and Plants of Limiting Global Warming to 1.5° Rather Than 2°." *Science* (May 18, 2018).
Weaver, J. E. *Prairie Plants and Their Environment*. Lincoln University of Nebraska Press, 1968.
Welti, Ellen A. R., et al. "Nutrient Dilution and Climate Cycles Underlie Declines in a Dominant Insect Herbivore." *Proceedings of the National Academy of Sciences of the United States of America* (March 31, 2020).
Wilsey, C. B. et al. "North American Grasslands & Birds Report." National Audubon Society (2019).

INDEX

Page numbers in italics refer to photos.

BENJAMIN VOGT is the owner of Monarch Gardens, a prairie-inspired design firm based in the Midwest, and author of the disruptive, call-to-action *A New Garden Ethic: Cultivating Defiant Compassion for an Uncertain Future*. Benjamin's award-winning writing and photography have appeared in some one hundred publications including *The American Gardener, Fine Gardening, Garden Design, Houzz, Midwest Living, Orion*, and a variety of literary and gardening books. As a sought-after speaker, he presents widely on artful and ecologically meaningful design for both wildlife and people, helping us to rethink pretty in a time of climate disruption. A native of Oklahoma and raised in Minnesota, Benjamin has an MFA from The Ohio State University and a PhD from the University of Nebraska. He lives in Lincoln on a re-prairied suburban lot with his wife and son.

The University of Illinois Press
is a founding member of the
Association of University Presses.

Text designed by Jim Proefrock
Composed in 10.5/14 Avenir 45 Book
with Avenir Condensed display
at the University of Illinois Press
Manufactured by Versa Press, Inc.

University of Illinois Press
1325 South Oak Street
Champaign, IL 61820-6903
www.press.uillinois.edu